Get a BACKBONE, Principal:

5 Conversations Every School Leader Must Have Right Now!

by Jill Jackson

outskirtspress
DENVER, COLORADO

The opinions expressed in this manuscript are solely the opinions of the author and do not represent the opinions or thoughts of the publisher. The author has represented and warranted full ownership and/or legal right to publish all the materials in this book.

Get a Backbone, Principal
5 Conversations Every School Leader Must Have Right Now!
All Rights Reserved.
Copyright © 2013 Jill Jackson
v3.0

Cover Photo by Sprague Minger. All rights reserved - used with permission.

This book may not be reproduced, transmitted, or stored in whole or in part by any means, including graphic, electronic, or mechanical without the express written consent of the publisher except in the case of brief quotations embodied in critical articles and reviews.

Outskirts Press, Inc.
http://www.outskirtspress.com

ISBN: 978-1-4787-1270-1

Outskirts Press and the "OP" logo are trademarks belonging to Outskirts Press, Inc.

PRINTED IN THE UNITED STATES OF AMERICA

For Little Punky, Soph and G. And for all of the other kids in our schools who deserve to be taught well so that they, too, can be stars…

Table of Contents

1   A Backbone Is Born 1

2   You, Yourself and You 13

3   The Instructional Coach 26

4   The Teaching Staff 43

5   The Teaching Teams 59

6   The Most Resistant Teacher 74

7   So What's Next? 88

8   Resources 91

Acknowledgements 109

1
A Backbone Is Born

I second-guessed myself on whether to title this book series "Get a Backbone!" – it is a little forward after all. But when I review everything I see in real life schools, it all comes down to this: *Excellent principals who get positive results have skills, but more importantly, they have a backbone! And they use it.*

Now, don't mistake having a backbone for rude, mean and "out-to-fire-everyone" kind of leadership. In fact, principals that lead with a backbone are some of the most beloved and highly revered leaders I've seen in action – they're the kind of leaders that folks will move schools just to work with. They're the kind of leaders that the staff wants to go above and beyond for. This isn't to say that their staff members don't roll their eyes after the staff meeting and whisper in the hallways and say, "Ugh! Why do the other schools get to work in their rooms in the afternoon and we have to go to a staff meeting? Our principal is so…mean!"

Principals with backbone have high standards – and they hold everyone accountable to them. Having high standards for all of their staff members and holding everyone accountable to those standards breeds confidence and purpose. And the cool thing? In the end, those same teachers who roll their eyes at the expectations are the same darn ones who stand proudly as they receive an award from the Superintendent for radically improving their scores or winning a national academic excellence award.

That's the thing: *When you principal with a backbone, you get results. Every time.*

I've seen it in my work with schools that are working really hard to close the achievement gap: principals who are clear about their expectations and make it their sole mission to protect and carry out the plan alongside their teachers, build a results-thinking staff. They work with the kind of staff that thinks first about what is best for the education of their kids. They're the kind of staff that you overhear talking about "our kids" – not "my kids." The principal's backbone supports the work and the staff expects it. The staff can borrow their principal's backbone when they are faced with a tough call. For example, let's imagine a few staff members are at a training conference that the district has paid for, and some of them from another school want to leave after lunch – not returning to the conference. If the principal of their colleagues' staff has a backbone, the teachers can use that as an excuse and say, "I would love to leave, but you know if Felicia finds out that we didn't stay all day, we're dust!" That's what I call "borrowing the backbone!"

I'm sure I don't need to point out that when you focus on the students instead of the adults, the quality of teaching is exponentially increased, right? Well, it is. Every time.

You may be wondering, "Now why should I listen to this Jill Jackson anyway?" (Believe me, I wonder the same thing sometimes.) Well, I've spent the better part of a decade working in the lowest performing schools, walking alongside them, pushing and shoving them, telling it like it is, getting them organized around their purpose, and all of the other things that come with school improvement. The most interesting part of the work is that, in most cases, it is not the district's or school's choice to bring me in – their funding sources have indicated that they need some sort of technical on-the-ground support. And then I show up! I could write a book about what I've seen – the good, the bad and the truly ugly. But one thing I know for sure and without exception is this: *without a leader who has a plan, and a backbone, there will be little long term improvement.*

What schools should really be looking at is not whether they can improve their scores, but whether they can *keep them there.*

This book is ultimately designed to be an encouragement and resource for folks who need a boost to move straight to getting the work done in real life schools. While I appreciate (and devour) the research books and how-tos on school reform, we don't need another one – especially from me. What we need is a realistic, step-by-step breakdown of what an ol' ordinary principal should do tomorrow to improve scores.

In my quest to find out what backbone-having principals with great results are really doing all day, I watched them in their natural state (in their schools) while they worked with their staff to improve their performance. I studied, but I also cajoled, fretted over them, pushed and shoved them. I held their hands when they thought they just might die having the hard conversations. I gave pep talks, and also acted as resident punching bag. And where I saw excellent backbone-fortified leadership, I saw results. Every time.

And here's what I found that led me to this whole backbone theory:

1. **Principals who lead with a backbone**…have a plan

2. **Principals with a backbone**…work the plan

3. **Principals with a backbone**…know that resistance to the plan is normal and not the end of the world

4. **Principals with a backbone**…are sometimes intimidated and overwhelmed, but they remember their plan and work it anyway

5. **Principals with a backbone**…aren't worried about "doing it perfectly"

6. **Principals with a backbone**…are always walking, talking and just "being" with their staff

Backbone-leading principals are doing things that other non-backbone-leading principals aren't. Those successful principals don't have superior skills or more in-depth training, they're just working their plan in spite of everything that presents itself as a roadblock.

Oh yeah, I've seen my fair share of principals who waffle about the plan, or are swayed by the latest fad and come back from every conference with the next greatest thing that they have to try right now! They wear out their staff, people stop believing that what they say actually does have instructional power and, ultimately, the staff thinks more about their plight (out of confusion and frustration) than about the students.

Now, just having backbone doesn't mean that you'll look up and find that all of your kids are miraculously performing above benchmark. You've got to *do* something with that backbone – lean into it and rely on it to accomplish some very strenuous instructional work at your school.

Side note: I use the word "strenuous" to describe the work to be done because it's not whether you have a school improvement plan – nearly all of them are identical – but whether a district or school is working the plan at a level of intensity that they never have before. Successful schools are made successful because they work with more intention and intensity than their lesser-performing counterparts.

It is common that I am met with a "these-are-great-ideas-but-you-don't-know-our-plight" kind of attitude. If I only had a nickel for every time I've heard, "You don't know how unsupportive our parents are," or "You don't know how messed up our schedule is," or "Our bus schedule dictates our instructional schedule – you have no idea," or "You don't know our Board – they're crazy!" Well, if you're reading this book with that kind of thought, I encourage you to lay it aside for a minute and think about this: Our job is to make improvement in learning happen *in spite of* all of this. I promise it works – I've seen it happen again and again.

The first place to start is to get a very clear, very simple instructional goal. Without an instructional goal, this book will be useless to you and you'll be "talking just to talk" during these conversations you'll have.

One of the school districts I worked with was having real trouble getting organized and focused in its work, and it was really frustrating to all the leaders. It seemed like they were trying everything and nothing was working. So, I handed out index cards and asked them to write down the district's three instructional goals for the school year, and to write them in the plainest English they could. Then they flipped the index card over and wrote what their individual school goals were related to the district goals.

Do you know what? *One hundred percent* of the school and district leaders in the room wrote something different for the district goals – in fact, they were nowhere near each other on what they thought the district goals were. And the flipped side of the card? Each school site had different instructional goals and several principals said that they couldn't name their goals.

I didn't have anything to say – the writing was on the wall.

So, guess where we started? With getting really clear on *one goal*.

Folks started to get frustrated with me, and one of the principals pulled me aside during the break and said things like, "You know, I think it's great that we're picking one goal and all, but I've got a school improvement plan and an RtI plan that has a total of 38 goals that we have to meet this year, so I've got to move much faster than just one goal." I get it – I've been there, but I also know that just the simple act of setting a bunch of goals does not increase the likelihood that we're going to actually get anything of value accomplished!

Now I know you probably can't relate, but it's a lot like dieting. As I consult my 50-plus books on weight loss, they all have one thing in common: if you want to lose weight, start small. For example, stop drinking regular soda. Or consider cutting out late night snacks. The problem is, when I'm highly motivated or under the gun because I have a big event coming up, and I need to fit into a not-so-big dress for the event, I tend to overdo it. I get motivated to cut my calories down to 1,200 and I decide that I'm never, ever, ever, ever again going to eat bread. And, while I'm at it, I'll cut out all carbs. Forever.

If you catch up to me a few days later, I'm so dang hungry that I end up sliding so far back, I'm worse off than when I started! Can you relate?

So, as soon as you go judging those principals and 'tsk-tsking' about how they should have focus, I want you to stop and think for a minute. What would you answer if I asked you these questions: Would *your* staff be able to have the school's goals roll off their tongue? Can you confidently spout off the district's instructional goals for this year?

I challenge you to take a stack of index cards to your next staff or team meeting and ask your staff to jot down what they believe is the school's primary instructional goal for this school year. Then, have the teachers jot down on the reverse side their instructional goal for their classroom this year. Give them only one minute to jot this down anonymously – this shouldn't be an over-thought task – either they know it or they don't. Bring the cards to your next leadership team meeting and have the team sort them into the patterns that they see. If the responses are pretty random, then you know that folks are confused about the message. If there's little written, it signals that there really is no message. If the responses are in line with the other instructional goals that you've set and carried out, pat yourself on the back!

The real deal is that most school improvement plans are built upon the very same foundational ideas: student engagement, behavior management, direct teaching, data analysis and decision-making, instructional planning and teaming. By focusing on just one of these areas, you will be able to cross off many of your school improvement "to do" items. Going small to go big (also called "starting small") is a very logical way to attack school improvement one step at a time. And the most awesome by-product is that you'll build incredible confidence among your staff. Successful principals leverage staff confidence to power through their other goals.

You'll notice that I reference "improving the quality of teaching" in every chapter of this book. The reason the phrase "quality of teaching" appears so many times is to remind you that, when all is said and done, *if your efforts have not improved the quality of the instruction, then your efforts have not produced much.*

Most school improvement books spend 90 percent of the time talking about what the district should do about school reform, how the principal should complete a 30-step reflection document to get better results in her role, and how the perfect lesson plan should be birthed. Few books focus on how to improve a school through increasing the quality of instruction in the classrooms and to the kids. If we are going to close the achievement gap, increase the test scores or see that our work has a measureable and actual impact on students, then at the heart of every one of our conversations has to be this: *How will this help us improve our quality of teaching as we are standing before our students and delivering the content?*

The conversations in this book are built around just that that: improving the quality of the instructional delivery.

We should not be focused on whether there's work going on in schools, rather we have to be most concerned with whether it is the right work – the work that is aligned with your instructional goals. So much time is spent on removing roadblocks to reach the goals, and successful schools know that as they prioritize the work on the quality of teaching, many of the roadblocks are removed – simply because they are focused on what instructional improvements they will make. That's the thing: roadblocks are removed when you focus on something other than the roadblocks themselves. In fact, if you're spending more time on what *won't* work, you will never see what *will* work.

If you're looking for a resource that uses big words and big formalized ideas on school improvement, then I'll bet you'll be disappointed in this book. I've written this book from a down-and-dirty perspective – from my knowledge of what really happens in schools. My hope is that you have a sense of humor as you read it because, while everything in it is absolutely true and factual, some of it is written a bit tongue-in-cheek.

I'm most inspired by regular principals who make a choice to do things differently with the staff they have, in the time they have, and with the resources they have. They aren't waiting for the Promised Land to arrive on their campuses, they're getting down to business right now. If you're not one of those principals now, I hope that by the end of the book, you realize that you have everything you need *right now* to become a highly successful principal. There's no need to wait any longer because the time to do so doesn't get any better than this moment.

So, now it's your turn. Your very first exercise. Yay! If you're anything like me, you won't do this exercise because you think it's not really meant to be done and it's only in theory that you need to complete it. But, I really want you to do it – you'll get a bigger payoff if you do, I promise.

So take a deep breath, grab the nearest pen or pencil and let's get started.

These three questions are going to help you map a very clear pathway to your main instructional goal and will become the focus of your actions following each chapter.

Paring Down My Instructional Focus

Question 1: *What is the one thing that is getting in the way of instructional power in most of the classrooms on your campus?*

_____

_____

Question 2: *What is the instructional practice (the "doing" of the teaching) that your staff has received the most professional development on and in which they are closest to becoming proficient?*

_____

_____

Question 3: *What is the one instructional practice that, if implemented regularly in every classroom on your campus, would increase the instructional impact?*

_____

_____

Now you want to take this information and craft it into an instructional goal. Your goal should incorporate these pieces:

- Why the change is necessary?
- Very specifically what the change or action is
- The measuring tool or the how you'll measure it
- Your timeline for implementation

For example, an instructional goal for a school that has students dealing with many behavior issues that either end up in your office and/or get in the way of instruction might be:

Currently, we recognize that teachers are often having to redirect behaviors, repeat directions for a task 3-4 times and are resorting to shushing students as they are instructing. This is causing us to lose many instructional minutes each day. To combat our problem, we will implement an "all eyes on me" rule in every classroom that will require the students to be looking directly at the teacher with no talking as the teacher gives directions. By January 17th, we will have 100% "eyes on the teacher" during direct instruction.

Now some folks will say, "Wait a minute – we need to increase twenty-four points on the state test this year and your instructional goal is having all eyes on the teacher? You've got to be kidding me!" They're skeptical about such a seemingly small goal having such big impact. Heck – even *you* might be skeptical! But what you have to remember is that a goal such as the "all eyes on me" is going to have an impact on so many facets of the teaching – more than you probably realize. Here's just a small list of how the above goal has tentacles in other, very important instructional areas:

- Time management – Teachers no longer have to repeat directions, etc.

- Instructional minutes – We have *gained* actual instructional minutes because we spend more time teaching, practicing and giving feedback than repeating and redirecting
- Behavior management – We are no longer wasting instructional minutes on behavioral concerns and students get what it "feels" like to be in control and respectful of their teacher
- Increased stamina – Kids are able to "hang in there" and keep their focus until the end of the lesson
- Continuity of instruction – We limit stops and starts, which allows the lesson to gain momentum which, in turn, allows the instructional intensity level to increase

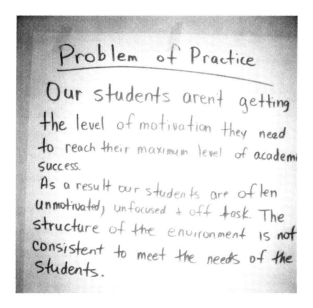

Here is a real-life example from a principal just like you:

You are so much closer to defining your backbone as a leader – it begins right here, with focus.

When it's all said and done and you've read all 3,041 "school improvement" books on Amazon (I checked!), you'll probably realize what I have realized: *backbone-having principals constantly have pointed and purposeful conversations with their staff members* – both casually and formally.

What they talk about, how often they talk about it and with whom they talk is the key to their success.

Those ongoing conversations are the backbone (pun intended!) of this book. My dream for you is that by the end of this book, you are more confident in purposely conversing about the work of your school with your staff than before you started reading. I can spend fifteen minutes with a principal during a casual interaction with a teacher and determine the power of his leadership – that's how power-packed these conversations are.

Yes, I know, you have a zillion things to accomplish on your School Improvement Plan. I know, you're out of the school constantly for training. Yep, I know you have a crabby parent or two waiting to see you at the end of the day. Uh huh, the reports are keeping you up and running 'til midnight every night. All these things are true, no doubt.

But in the end, successful principals who lead with a backbone, spend important time talking with the folks who carry out the mission with them: the teaching staff. Your greatest asset in your school is your teaching staff, and in order to be successful and close the achievement gap, you must lead them with purpose, show up boldly for the mission and remember that you do, indeed, have a backbone.

In fact, sometimes all of us have to reach back and feel that hard, bumpy thing running the length of the back – it's the backbone. It's always there, but we've got to use it, exercise it and remember to lean into it while we're in the trenches doing good work.

2
You, Yourself and You

Stop wearing your wishbone where your backbone ought to be.
- Elizabeth Gilbert

The Scene: You're sitting at your umpteenth district meeting this week – the good thing is that you got there early and squired one of the cushy board room chairs, so at least you'll be comfortable in the mire that is the weekly leadership meeting. The talk is yet again about how you need to improve the scores and how another "national consultant" has figured out how you should do that.

In reality, you wish you were back at your office working on the zillions of things that are piling up on your desk by the minute…in fact you pray that there's a (minor) emergency that will justify you heading back to school before the meeting is over. You keep checking your phone and wondering why your secretary, who texts and calls you constantly when you are in truly important meetings, is failing to bail you out this time! You're staring at your phone *willing* it to ring or beep just so that you can step out of the room.

But it doesn't.

And you leave yet another district meeting with a list of fifty things that needed to be done yesterday. And thirty-seven things that need to be done today. And 120 things that need to be done tomorrow.

You're thinking about that new math program that your teachers just had training on and how half of the information in this meeting today is totally opposite of what the trainer just taught your teachers. So this means that you're going to have to go back to the staff *again* and tell them that what they heard before isn't what you want them to do now, and that it really isn't your fault that they got the wrong information – it's "the district" that's causing all of this confusion.

So, you head back into the school where the office staff accosts you with the super important (and not-so-super-important) message slips from folks who have called and need to talk to you about this and that.

And well, it's almost lunch time and you've been covering a duty for the teachers, because since the funding shift you've been down two instructional aides and in order for the teachers to get their lunch break that the union requires them to have, you have to cover. You actually like it because it's the one time of the day when you don't have to be on the phone or in a meeting, but as you man the lunch trays and overflowing garbage cans, more message memos are piling on top of the other ones on your desk.

Looks like another night of getting your *actual* job done after everyone has gone home for the night. It's your fourth night this week that you won't be home until 9:00 p.m.

The Analysis: You're being "done to" in your role as leader. You're controlled by the job and exhausted by it. You sit at meetings and walk into the office and wait for the other shoe to drop – and it usually does. You are not controlling the messages to the teachers, but going back on your word so many times makes you look weak and wishy-washy when, in reality, you *do* have some great ideas to implement that you *know* will actually work. It's time to take a deep breath, gear up and be disciplined in a "Let's Do This!" mindset and recommit to your purpose.

You had a purpose, a reason for becoming a leader. Remember that? You just need to re-discover it.

I'm going to make this really easy on you: don't tell anyone. Just start acting like you have a backbone right now.

Yep – just start. Like right now. Put down the book and start. I mean it!

Where you might have waffled before, just be decisive. While you might have waited for the last late arrival to your staff meeting, just start on time. In a situation where you might have asked for a ton of feedback, ask one trusted colleague and make that decision. Try saying "no." Try saying, "Yes!" Just start.

I have seen very well-read and highly-trained principals lose major growth opportunities with their staff because they're waiting for the "right time" or "buy-in." We need to be clear on this idea as we're prepping for a powerful instruction-focused future: many a plan has been stymied and steamrolled by leaders who were waiting around for "buy-in."

In my experience, "building buy-in" is a fancy term used to cover for a skittish leader – one who is afraid of fallout from tough, instructional decisions that must be made. One hundred percent of the time, buy-in is built *while* we're doing the work of improving our schools. It is built within the context of the work – not separate from it. So, if you're thinking, "Gee, I've got to make some big instructional decisions at my school, but I need to warm the staff up to the idea for a bit," you're missing the boat, buddy! And I want you on the boat, not waving from the shore.

What Principals with a Backbone Know About Self-Talk

Some might say that people who talk to themselves are a little crazy. As a person who regularly converses with herself, I disagree. And I hope you do, too – and here's why: I'll bet if I followed you around and logged every time you had to make a decision in one school day, the total would exceed one hundred. Do you agree? Heck – it might be in the two hundreds!

Whether it's deciding on whether or not to reschedule a meeting because one of the team members is absent, or whether to have the Breakfast with Santa on the same Saturday as the Fireman's Pancake Breakfast, or who should be the school representative at the Safe School Committee meeting at the district office on Thursday – you're making decisions all day long. And you need to go beyond just gut checks and knee-jerk reactions in making those decisions – especially when they impact the quality of instruction.

Here's where the talking to yourself comes in…

Savvy principals know that the decisions that they make are going to set the tone for other decisions to come. They also know that by simply making decisions, other less important decisions tend to just go away. And most importantly, powerful principals know the staff is watching their every move, analyzing the decisions and deducing what is important or not important based upon these decisions. This is where you have to train yourself to talk through the outcome of even the teensiest decision before you pull the trigger.

Powerful principals making decisions do some good ol' fashioned self-talk around these types of questions:

- Does this decision have an impact on the heart of instruction positively or negatively or not at all?

- Does this decision get in the way or give the impression of interfering with our instructional goals?
- Does my decision impact the instructional minutes in the day? Am I setting a precedent that I do not value those minutes if I allow this activity to interfere?
- Does my message conflict with professional development that the teachers have had? How will I reconcile this?
- Am I piling another thing on the teachers that will unnecessarily overwhelm them? Can it possibly wait or is the time right?
- Who can I run this decision by prior to rolling it out to the staff? Who can give me real-time feedback on this?
- Is this a decision that even has to be made or can I let it go?
- What is the timeline for making this decision? Can I delay it for a more opportune time?
- Am I falling for a fad-like trick or is this decision based upon solid research and sound practice?
- Should I run this by the Leadership Team or is this my decision to make alone?
- What will it look like when I implement this decision? Do I like the picture I see in the long run?
- Are there others who have made this decision before me? I wonder what kind of input they can provide.
- Do I need more data before I make the decision or do I have enough for a "yes" or "no" right now?
- Does it just plain "make sense?"

I worked with a fantastic principal who turned around a less-than-fantastically-performing school and she reports this about the art of making a decision, *"I try to delay making decisions by at least fifteen minutes because I find that people who pressure me to make quick decisions have an agenda. They are using the tactic of a quick decision to get me to AVOID thinking things through – and it's usually for their benefit. On the other hand, if I delay decision-making too long, I look weak. And one thing I'm not is weak! So, I have my go-to questions in my head, kind of like my checklist that helps me funnel the question or request and then I make it like I mean business. Even if I'm slightly unsure whether the decision is the best, I make it with gusto – like I mean it."*

What a powerful leader! She delays the decision long enough to run it through her mental checklist, but she really *means it* once she makes the decision. She also checks to make sure that, even though something sounds like a good decision, it lines up with the school's instructional focus. Too many good things can turn out to be a bad thing. Bottom line? She doesn't mess around. (An interesting fact: She has teachers on a waiting list to come and work at her school.)

That's backbone, folks! Making a decision and meaning it.

So This Is What a Backbone-Having Conversation Sounds Like:

I'm going to imagine that I am a principal who has completed the first exercise of brainstorming my school's instructional goals and I realize that I have too many – in fact I can name about fifteen – different focus areas that I've shared with the staff in the past four months. Here's what the "my-backbone-is-firmly-embedded" conversation with myself might sound like:

"Okay girl, so you've gotten yourself into a little jam here. Time to dig your way out and get down to business. First off, you identified that your primary instructional goal and the one that would absolutely transform each classroom is to increase the <u>amount</u> of instructional planning that

the teachers do. We also want to improve the <u>quality</u> of their planning.

Next is to share with the staff that you have over-committed to goals and that you're sure you've confused and overwhelmed them in the process. Just admit it – they'll appreciate it. Then you need to re-commit to the instructional goal of increasing planning time and quality. Oh, and be sure to tell them why. Then <u>get their input</u> – see how they're feeling and reacting. Then take this information to the Leadership Team and ask them this question: "Guys, how are we going to gradually increase the time we spend in instructional planning and also how we actually do the planning?" And just listen.

You know you have a tendency to just barge ahead – and that's what landed you smack dab into this problem to begin with. Start by just listening. Then gather the information and ask the team where they think we ought to start. Better yet, have the team go back to their grade levels and ask them where the weaknesses in their planning are and where they would like to start. You need to remember that this is why you have the darn Leadership Team to begin with!

Now it's time to tackle how you're going to undo some of the things that you've committed to doing. You're going to have to talk with Mr. Johnson about that joint PD day you agreed to – it sounded like a good idea and his enthusiasm was really contagious, but it directly conflicts with our instructional goal – it's "adding more" rather than streamlining the planning process. That gets me thinking about the fact that our grade level teaming agenda template is so full that we never get to everything on the agenda, let alone to planning next week's lessons! We've got to adjust and pare that agenda down so that we actually highlight our main instructional goal during those meetings.

But first things first. Start to script your notes to share at Tuesday's staff meeting about the instructional focus and 'going small to go big'. You can DO this – and you're not alone."

Tip: Visit Resource 1, 2 and 3 in the Resources section

Planning for *Your* Backbone-Having Conversation

So, it's that time now – the time where you commit to doing something small but powerful. You need to commit to taking an action or two that firmly connects to your instructional focus. This is it! These questions are designed to get you thinking about what you really want to see at your site – and will help you focus in on your 1-2 instructional goals.

Question 1: *What is my first thought when I ask myself this question: What is the #1 CONTROLLABLE inhibitor to our instructional success at our school?*

_____

_____

Question 2: *What is the #2 CONTROLLABLE inhibitor to our instructional success at our school?*

_____

_____

Question 3: *What is the one instructional-focus-type conversation I need to have in the next five days? With whom? What do I want the purpose of the conversation to be? Why is this conversation a priority?*

_____

_____

Question 4: *What is the one instructional-focus-type conversation I need to have in the next fifteen days? With whom? What do I want the purpose of the conversation to be? Why is this conversation a priority?*

_____

_____

Question 5: *What is my dream for my school? What do I want it to look like when we're operating on all cylinders? How is that different from our current mode of operation?*

_____

_____

Question 6: *Who can I get to support me and hold me accountable for this?*

_____

_____

Quit Putting Out Fires and Get To Your Powerful Purpose

Originally published on www.jackson-consulting.com on December 10, 2012

I would not be exaggerating if I said everywhere that I go educators are complaining about not having enough time. Here's what it sounds like…

From the principal: *I would LOOOOOVE to get into the classrooms more often, but I have so many behavioral issues that take up my time!*

From the coach: *I would LOOOOOVE to get in a debrief within 24 hours, but I have to finish up paperwork and go to so many trainings that I often end up giving feedback to teachers a week later!*

From teachers and teams: *We would LOOOOOVE to spend more time prepping for those lessons, but all of the other stuff that we have to do take so much time that the preparation and planning is my last step each week and I'm exhausted by the time I get there!*

What's the common denominator? They all would LOOOOOVE to do something!

Well, here's the deal: I LOOOOOVE to go get my nails done. In fact I did it yesterday! I love taking my book that has nothing to do with work. I love that they don't allow cell phones so there are no rings or pings or interruptions. I love to come out of the nail salon all shiny and new. I love the choices of colors. I just love it. (I know some of you are reading this and thinking…is she *really* going to talk manicures? Yes, she *really* is, but she'll get to a bigger point, so hang in there…)

And because I love it, I make sure I don't miss my appointment.

Let's take for example yesterday. I had an appointment at 5:00 p.m. It takes 15 minutes to drive to this particular nail place and sometimes parking is a challenge, so I knew I needed to leave at 4:30 from my house to get there in plenty of time.

So I **backtracked my tasks** so that I was done at 4:30 on the dot.

Because my nail appointment was important to me and I didn't want to miss it and have it overwhelmed by everything else.

I put my phone calls **on my calendar at SPECIFIC times** – not just on a to-do list.

I put my **email answering at a SPECIFIC time** – not just on a to-do list.

I put my writing **projects at SPECIFIC times** – not just on a to-do list.

I even put in a couple of 15 minute **breaks at SPECIFIC TIMES** – not just on a to-do list.

The thing is, I LOOOOOOVE a good to-do list, but I find that when I don't schedule my tasks out, the list gets a few things crossed off, but most of them remain at the bottom…especially the ones I don't want to do. So what does this have to do with putting out fires and manicures and all this mess?

If most educators cite *time* as a #1 or #2 inhibitor of getting things done that they know they should get done, and we know that we aren't going to just magically create more time, then the answer

to being frenzied and out of time all the time is managing our time differently.

Managing our time, I've found and seen in excellent and productive educators, is the difference between running around and putting out fires and *purposeful* work in our schools. Let me give you an example:

Say that you've scheduled your prep time for 7:00 a.m. - 7:45 a.m. (of course I know you need more time than this, but this is one chunk of time you've scheduled). You've actually *written it into* your calendar – so it's a date! **And along comes Suzy Q** and she LOOOOVES to talk…and talk…and talk. **Typically you shoot the breeze with Suzy Q** and when you're done, you think, "Ugh! I just wasted all of that time and I got nothing done!". (Does this sound at all familiar?)

You are now behind – and in "putting out fires" mode…you're in reactionary mode because now you feel under the gun.

(On a side note: "putting out fires" and "under the gun" – -neither *sound* real fun, do they?)

So let's rewrite this scenario:

You have scheduled time from 7:00 – 7:45 a.m. to prep for your upcoming lessons tomorrow and Wednesday. Suzy Q comes in and says, "Hey girl/guy! What's up?" and settles in for a nice, long chat… about *nothing*!

You can now say, "Hey Suz! Whew – I'm really busy! I've scheduled myself for some prep right now…go grab your books and come prep with me!" or "Hey Suz! You know, my schedule is really hounding me right now…I've got my prep time for tomorrow and Wednesday right now – let's sit together at lunch and get all caught up!"

It's these kinds of conversations that not only allow us to stay on track, but put other time-wasters (people and tasks) on notice that we aren't messing around anymore!

When we're under the gun and pushing the envelope, we are *reacting*. And oftentimes our most important tasks get pushed to the bottom of the list. And **both of these things make us feel like we're being managed, not managing.**

And I don't know about you, but I want to be **the manager, not the managed**!

So…what is this all about?

- It's about **taking control** of the time you have and getting down to business on the things that are important to our delivery of excellent instruction
- It's about **not being in reactionary, "putting out fires" mode** – because that mode means we're not doing our best work
- It's about **organizing our environment** so that we are optimized for doing our best, being our best and producing our best with the time we're given
- It's about **having a life** where the bag of papers to grade doesn't come home with you every single night because you've managed time poorly
- The cool thing? **Time management is also contagious for your kids**! They need to see it too!

So…where will you start?

3
The Instructional Coach

The leadership instinct you are born with is the backbone. You develop the funny bone and the wishbone that go with it.
– Elaine Agather

The Scene: You're walking through classrooms doing informal observations and you run into your instructional coach several times throughout the day. She's as busy as can be, running around helping grade level teams, copying and delivering some decodable books for the interventionist's latest reading group, and she reminds you that she'll be out for training for the next three days, so she'll see you next week.

You hear whisperings about the coach ("She's always in my room!" or "I never see her!" or "I wish I had her job – it looks so cushy!"), but you know that all this comes with the territory of having a coach – the job always looks way more glamorous than it really is. Kind of like *your* job!

Come to think of it, you have also heard grumblings from 5th grade teachers during their grade level team meetings. They're saying the coach isn't really helpful and sometimes sticks her nose in their business. They're also not a big fan of having someone who hasn't taught as long as they have in their classrooms giving advice. I mean, what does *she* know that they don't know after twenty-two years of teaching?

But it's been weeks, maybe even months, since you've met with the coach one-on-one and even though she's busy, you're not quite sure what she's working on every day. And quite honestly, you're so busy with the new math initiative that you haven't had the time to touch base. In fact, you've been thinking lately that ever since the budget cuts have hit your school, it might not be a bad idea to bring the coach back into an interventionist role. After all, that's what the teachers want and it kind of makes sense.

You know that a coach is an important part of a school, but to be quite honest, you're not quite sure what exactly you should be expecting of the coach everyday – and you really don't understand the whole "trust" issues and boundaries between what the teachers tell the coach and what the coach can/should tell you. Every time you ask her about what she's seeing in the classrooms, it's as if she's seen a ghost, and she figures out a reason to get out of the office real quick! And you're thinking, "What *is* it about being in a teacher's classroom together – is it such a bad thing?" It's not like you're asking her to fill out a formal evaluation of the teacher. If you don't get information from the coach, then what is the value of having one? It seems like you and your coach are ships passing in the night – and the results are pointing to the fact that you're not getting a big bang for your buck by having an instructional coach on site.

Gosh, turning the coach into an interventionist is sounding like a great decision, the more you think of it.

The Analysis: Your situation is a perfect example of "just because we have a coach on campus, doesn't mean that coaching is happening," and that has got to change…fast. Your coach makes it a priority to very purposefully steer clear of you – this signals that there are blurred roles between the coach and you. And that has also got to change…fast. When it seems like a coach would best be utilized back in the classroom "working with kids" rather than working to perfect the instruction "to the kids," that's typically a sign that the true value of the coaching role has either not been explored by you, or has not been embraced by the coach. When I see this in the field, it's common to find that the principal and coaches themselves are unclear about what coaching should look like. And that's yet another thing that has got to change…fast.

What you have here is this: confusion and misperception about the coach's role. The easiest way to bring the power back to the coaching role is to have a quick and private meeting with the coach to mull this question: *What does coaching look like when you're working at full tilt with the teachers?* By starting here, you will be able to air out exactly where the coach sees her work heading, and then also share what your priorities are for her in that role. It is common to find that the coach has received professional development on the coaching role and the principal has not. This can cause confusion or frustration, because the principal and coach, whose work should be closely tied, are coming from completely different perspectives on what coaching actually is. If this is the case, it is the time to air it out so that you stop sending mixed messages to your staff. So much resistance to coaching comes from teachers feeling like the coach is looking for one thing and the principals is looking for another, and the teachers are smack dab in the middle of the confusion. And it's likely that the "coach is evaluating me" comments crop up because the teachers are confused about what the coach's role really is.

Side note: It's at this point that I would lose my educational consultant license to practice if I didn't mention this: of course your coach's priorities and activities should be directly tied to your school's instructional focus area(s). There. I said it!

Once you and your coach are completely clear about what the role is and isn't, you owe it to your staff to hit the "reset" button and explain what coaching will look like from this point forward.

What Principals with Backbone Know About the Instructional Coach

Backbone-having principals realize that a strong, skilled coach on a mission is the best ally a leader can have on the road to closing the achievement gap. But a strong, skilled coach on a mission doesn't happen overnight – and they don't come out of the box that way! The principal must set up (and show up to) weekly meetings with the coach where they discuss what the instructional focus is, what the instruction is looking like out in the classrooms, what types of support opportunities the coach should be providing, and who is struggling with the instructional focus and might need more coaching time in the upcoming week. This is where the coach and principal work to tailor the professional development, determine the focus of next week's grade level team meetings, figure out which grade level should share successes at the next staff meeting, and choose which teachers needs more coaching time and extra focus. It's the "get on the same page" time that is essential for maximizing the coaching impact on the staff.

What principals on a mission also realize about coaching is that it's lonely – the coach is not quite principal and not quite teacher and they oftentimes feel like they don't fit anywhere. So, the weekly "touching-base" meetings are critical, not only for bringing purpose and clarity to the work, but they're necessary to build a connection between the coach's work, the principal's work and the instructional focus. The coach needs to be heard by you, needs to be able to bounce ideas off of you and even have you "bless" her next steps – especially when there is push-back and resistance. What they *don't* need is you blabbing to someone about what you've talked about during your meeting with them, or making reference to what the coach has referenced in private. These are trust killers and take a long time to recover from. But you already knew that, right?

Principals with backbone know that coaching is for every staff member – and they set this expectation clearly up front. One of the biggest inhibitors to coaches getting into the classrooms is a frustration about where to start. If you lead your coach to meet briefly with every teacher after you've set your instructional goal(s), and you let your staff know that this is mandatory for everyone, you will make your coach's job infinitely simpler. Strong leaders realize that it's the coach's job to tailor support to the skill level of the teacher, and clearing a path for coaches to approach every teacher is a major priority.

The coach's first "get-my-foot-in-the-door" question to teachers should be, "I know that Principal John has set increasing instructional engagement as our main goal – where do you see us starting to work on that in your classroom?" Without your focus and 'everyone gets coaching' message, the question becomes, "Where would you like to start?" Oftentimes without focus on a particular area of instruction, teachers will either stall the coach or they will choose something that they already know how to do because they can't think of anything else to focus on at that moment. This is not usually an act of resistance – it's an act of not knowing! Teachers thrive on substance and direction – and the coach must frame the work with teachers so that by working with the coach, the teacher is essentially preparing for the principal's next observation. Everything is linked back to that instructional goal and the principal's expectations of what the entire staff is held accountable to. A strong coaching setup ensures that there are few surprises throughout the coaching process and the teachers feel like there is more of a partnership and less of a "gotcha!" mentality.

Successful principals know that coaching should follow an agreed-upon format or shape – it is not random or led entirely by the teacher. Coaching is most successful when it occurs at the intersection of the teacher, coach and principal. You will get great results when it works like this: the principal sets the instructional goal to the staff and the coach and teacher commiserate on how to get the teacher 'coached up' to meet the principal's expectation. This roots the coaching in the instructional goals and gives it shape. Without a form and shape, it's nearly impossible to measure the impact of coaching on the staff.

Here's the big take-away: if we set up coaching properly from the beginning, let the teachers know exactly how coaching will be handled, what the focus of it will be, and that they know it's mandatory for everyone, there is much less resistance. The great thing is, even if you haven't set up the coaching cleanly and you're well into it, you can go back to your staff and repurpose how coaching will look from here on out.

Principals who lean into their backbone know that the flow of coaching should be typical and habitual – it should have a shape and structure that is repeated again and again. When we have a regular cycle of *how* we coach then the focus can be on *what* we coach. If the form of coaching is random, then teachers will spend their time thinking, "I wonder what's next?" rather than, "Oh, here are the two questions I want to ask the coach during the debriefing." I have seen schools keep coaching very free-form and a bit too loosey-goosey in an effort to make it more palatable for resistant teachers. And in these situations, teachers will often report back to me that they feel like they "don't know what they're supposed to do with the coach," they "don't know if they're doing coaching right" or, in the worst-case scenario, they "think coaching is a waste of time." Eek!

The coaching process should incorporate these three steps:

1. **Pre-conference:** The coach sets up a quick check-in with the teacher to determine the who, what, where, when, why and how of the coaching cycle. Specifically, what the coach and teacher will be looking for, what types of notes the coach will take, where the coach will sit, how the teacher should handle the students when the coach enters the classroom, and when the coach and teacher will debrief. The coach should pay particular attention to the style of coaching that will take place, should ask questions like: will we best meet our coaching goals by having me observe you and provide feedback? Have you observe me and reflect on what you saw? Observe another teacher who has mastered this technique and include them in the debriefing? Videotape the lesson and critique it together? Co-teach the lesson? Engage in side-by-side coaching where I give you feedback right on the spot during your lesson?

2. **Gathering the Data and Evidence:** This is where the teacher and coach do what they agreed to do during the pre-conference. This step should *not be confused as coaching* – not a lot of feedback is exchanged. This is simply a data-gathering step where the teaching takes place and the note taking begins.

3. **Debriefing:** This is the heart of the coaching and where the reflection, analysis and feedback happen. Without this step, there is little to no coaching. Period. Successful principals measure and monitor that the debriefings are actually happening. During the debriefing, the coach asks questions like: what did you think was successful in the lesson? How do you know? If you were to do this lesson again, what might you

change and why? Did the lesson turn out like you planned? Was there anything that surprised you?

The coach should be set up by the principal to be free to give specific feedback and recommendations based upon the data they picked up in Step 2 (Gathering the Data and Evidence). You must very clearly establish with the teachers that the coach will be giving specific, corrective feedback so that they are expecting it. I want you to hear this loud and clear: *every single debriefing should end with an agreed upon action from the teacher.* Without it, coaching is just another item on the list of things for teachers to do and you will not see impact on the quality of instruction on your campus.

While coaching has a form, it is definitely not "one size fits all." The following chart will help you and your coach see how, while following the three steps in the coaching process, there is still plenty of room for tailoring the support to each teacher.

Bringing Form and Focus to the Coaching Role, Pre-Conference	
During the Pre-Conference, the coach might ask...	<ul><li>Tell me how you're structuring your time as you teach XYZ</li><li>What lessons are you presenting?</li><li>What strategies are you implementing with the intensive/strategic/benchmark students? How is that going?</li><li>What parts of the lesson are a "slam dunk" and which leave you feeling less than accomplished?</li><li>I know that we focused on XYZ previously. How is your continued implementation of those techniques going? What areas can use further refining just like we did with XYZ?</li><li>I know that you were focused on bring Johnny, Juan and Emilie to benchmark. How is their progress? What have you tried? What do you need further support in?</li><li>Tell me a little more about…</li><li>Let me see if I understand…</li><li>Tell me more about…</li><li>I'm wondering…</li><li>I talked with Mrs. Jones about XYZ yesterday. How are you feeling about that area?</li></ul>

Bringing Form and Focus to the Coaching Role, Gathering the Data and Evidence	
While the coach gathers the data…	**As coach observes teacher, the coach will:** - Communicate care - Be unobtrusive - Use teacher's manual to follow lesson - Establish ahead of time where you will sit - Avoid interrupting lesson, unless negotiated during pre-conference - Observe exactly what was agreed upon in pre-conference **The following should be pre-negotiated:** - The level of participation expected from the coach during the lesson - If the teacher is observing the coach, what materials or lesson plans the teacher should follow - If the teacher is observing the coach, the coach should provide the teacher with 2-3 main focus points ("I'd like you to keep track of how long my transitions from A to B take" or "As you observe the lesson, watch for my scaffolding of the reading for the strategic readers in your class") - The coach shares the debriefing questions: "When we meet, we'll discuss what you found as far as transitions and how I scaffolded for the strategic students. I'll also ask you what you would do differently and what you'll try in your classroom based upon the observation"

Bringing Form and Focus to the Coaching Role, Debriefing	
Debriefing	**Reflecting on the instruction, the coach will ask the teacher:** • How did you think the lesson went? • What would you do differently? Why? • What triggered that thought? • How is this different from how you might have delivered the lesson? • Tell me what you thought when… • How do you know that…? • What I hear you saying is… • What were you surprised about? • What can you imagine us focusing on next? • This leads me to think that we should take a look at… **Reflecting on the coaching process** • How can we improve upon our coaching exchanges in the future? • What type of coaching technique might be even more supportive of you? (Side-by-side coaching, observation of another teacher with coach, data study meeting, observation of coach teaching, mirror coaching, co-teaching a lesson)

Tip: Visit Resource 4 and 5 in the Resources section

So This Is What a Backbone-Having Conversation Sounds Like:

"Juanita, I'd like to talk with you about your coaching work and spend time bringing focus and clarity to the work that you'll do with the teachers from here on out. I appreciate that you're spending an incredible amount of time with the teachers in the classrooms, and that a lot of your time is spent gathering materials and solving scheduling and data issues that arise – you truly are a resource for the teachers and I know how much they appreciate you. What I have noticed about your time coaching is that it appears that you have been putting out fires more than purposely coaching them on their teaching to our instructional goals. I take full responsibility for the fact that I did a pretty weak job of setting up your role and I need to fix that with the staff. My commitment is to realign your work with the instructional goals that we set at last week's staff meeting so that ninety percent of your work is in the classrooms with the teachers working on carrying out those goals.

I'd like to start by establishing together what your role is and what it will look like when you are deep in the heart of your coaching. What I see that we need to work toward is a weekly meeting between the two of us where we take twenty minutes to determine who our focus teachers are for this week, what coaching was accomplished last week, then take a look at upcoming instructional expectations and plan for how you will carry out the coaching of those expectations. Does that sound like a plan?

Yes, I know that you're worried about appearing like you're evaluative in your role if we have weekly meetings behind closed doors, but I am going to be very up-front with the teachers about our meetings and the purpose for them: that we calibrate what we are looking for in the classrooms and get organized, so there is no gap between the work you're doing and what I'm looking for when I observe in classrooms. I think the staff will welcome us working to the same goal – I'll bet it'll be a relief for them.

The one topic that I'd like to discuss during our first weekly meeting is the cycle of coaching. Right now, I believe you are set up to work with the teachers who ask for help or those who have some sort of 'fire' that needs extinguishing. I need you to know that your coaching power is going to rest on a conscious effort to stay very tightly focused on our instructional goals and I'd like to work with you on organizing your coaching cycle more succinctly on those goals. At next week's meeting, let's determine which teachers need the most support, based upon our observations, and prioritize them to the top of your calendar for that week.

So, what do you think? Do you think bringing shape and focus to your role will allow you to have greater impact on the quality of instruction in our classrooms? What is intimidating about this adjustment to your role? What do you feel confident in around this change? Does this solve real roadblocks that you experience?

Planning for Your Backbone-Having Conversation:

Question 1: *What is the current state of your coaching program right now? What are the top three tasks you see your coach engaging in most regularly? Are these in line with your instructional goals?*

_____

_____

Question 2: *When you think honestly about your past setup for coaching, did you set high expectations for 100 percent participation, or were there holes in who should participate in coaching and who didn't have to?*

_____

_____

Question 3: *What kind of information or record-keeping do you need to see from the coach in order for you to measure the progress and success of the coach's work? What will be your accountability points?*

_____

_____

Question 4: *How will you prioritize the coaching? Who are the specific teachers who need extra coaching time? Which teachers don't think they need help, but would really benefit from regular coaching? What data will you use to determine this?*

_____

_____

Question 5: *Are there specific teachers who are resisting working with the coach? Who are they and what message do you want to give them?*

_____

_____

Question 6: *What are the three main points you need to make to the staff about the re-focusing of the coaching role? What do you need to prepare them for?*

_____

_____

Prioritizing the Coaching Role to Maximize Teacher Support

Originally published on www.jackson-consulting.com
on July 5, 2012

There is no doubt that if I could create time for coaches I would be a very rich woman.

And if I were very wealthy, I probably would be writing this blog from Bora Bora, taking an excessive amount of breaks to jump off the hut into the water, and grab a shell that would contain a one pound black pearl that the man who fans me with palm fronds would string onto a necklace…WAIT!

Ahem.

Um.

Let me start again here.

Well good morning, fine educators! I am so pleased that you have chosen to join me here on this fine morning/afternoon/evening as we delve into the art of instructional coaching and how to mentor.

Okay. So that's a little overboard, too. I'm a gal of extremes…so sue me!

Really what I'd like to share with you is how to create more time instructional coaching by prioritizing your calendar and the work that you do. It really will help you grasp how you will spend quality time with the teachers who need most support.

So, here are some powerful but easy-to-implement actions in prioritizing the instructional coaching role. I'm excited for you to make every moment with your teachers count – for them and for you.

Tip One: Privately organize (so as to not be evaluative) the teachers in your coaching cadre by intensive, strategic and benchmark in relation to how they're performing on your school's instruction focus areas.

Directly coach and have contact with the intensive teachers once a week, the strategic teachers at least once every two weeks and the benchmark/advanced teachers at least once a month.

Tip Two: Create a coaching calendar to give focus to your instructional coaching.

You are less likely to be pulled to substitute at the last minute for an absent teacher, attend a meeting on behalf of the principal or be pulled to fix the copier (ha!) when you are moving around your school with purpose.

If people ask you to do something that might be outside of your position, you can say, "I would love to help – but I'm booked in classrooms until 9:30, I'll check back with you then and I'd be glad to help!"

What you'll find is that they will have long moved on by the time you check back.

Tip Three: Schedule the debriefing of the coaching cycle during the pre-conference. You will spend much less time chasing down the teacher in the end. When you honor the teacher's time, too, you strengthen the relationship.

Tip Four: Listen. Really listen. Oftentimes, you'll be able to have "coachable moments" with a teacher that will lead you more informally into the instructional coaching cycle.

Use these times to pre-conference and before you know it, you're right back into the coaching cycle and getting that teacher feedback and notes.

Look for natural extensions of coaching in less formal settings – they can be your most fertile coaching locations.

What do you think? Can you see how these little tips all add up to more coaching time? I certainly hope you can see it, because I have so much evidence from the field that they *do* work!

4
The Teaching Staff

A lot of people are afraid to tell the truth, to say no. That's where toughness comes into play. Toughness is not being a bully. It's having backbone."
–Robert Kiyosaki

The Scene: You are holding your monthly staff meeting on an early release day and you routinely go through the regular agenda items detailing what time the teachers need to show up to sign their insurance forms, when the submissions for the upcoming art faire are due to the school secretary, and how there have been problems in the boys bathroom with the toilets getting clogged, so the new school rule is that only one student at a time can enter the bathroom.

You scan the room and notice that the usual suspects are late coming back from lunch again (they say there was a big back-up in the drive-thru line), two of your teachers are missing from the meeting because they scheduled dentist appointments for this afternoon, and you see three teachers grading papers while you're talking.

Just another regular staff meeting!

After the meeting, about eight teachers come up to talk with you. Mr. Jones, the one stuck in the drive-thru line, says that he doesn't have the right paper for the art faire submissions and where would he find it anyway? Ms. Johnson lets you know that she is going to be absent during the testing window and so she will need coverage. Mr. Pinkny informs you that there were six referrals from yesterday and that he has a 'really bad class' this year, and something needs to be done. Mrs. Shower says that her instructional aide hasn't been showing up until 10 minutes after the small groups have begun, and so her kids are going nuts during small group time because they don't have a teacher, and you need to "deal with" her aide right away. They have been missing their aide for four weeks. Mr. Heatherton showed you his mid-year test scores and it appears as though nine kids slipped from benchmark to well below benchmark, and he thinks that seven of these nine should be tested for Special Ed.

Ms. Pembroke wants to set up a time to talk to you about whether she really needs to attend the grade level team meetings because she's "not getting much from them," and since they only last twenty minutes anyway, could she use that time to pull a small group of struggling kids? Mr. Langston would like to know if he could keep his own kids during reading intervention because he doesn't feel like the kids are getting anything out of the interventionists group. He hasn't really looked at the data, he says, but he just has a feeling that it's not going well. And finally Mrs. Wagner asks if she can talk to you privately because she's going through some personal problems and she's having trouble getting to school on time because her daycare has fallen through.

You head back to your office with a headache and you're met by two teachers (who were grading papers during the meeting) who wanted to know, "What did you say again about the art faire deadline?"

The Analysis: You need to regain control. It's time to set a higher standard for professionalism – and then require that your staff follow through. There appears to be general apathy toward the real instructional work that is necessary at the school. You are lacking the extreme focus and energy on the teaching-related tasks, and those are the tasks that will actually produce the results that you desire. You might think, "I want to make my school instruction-centered, but we have so much other 'junk' that gets in the way. And I have no control over that junk and have to share it at the meeting!"

If you really analyze the concerns that are brought to you after the meeting, you realize that most of them should be discussed *during* the meeting. The lagging data, the Special Ed referrals, the lack of focus of instructional aides, classroom management – these are the tasks that, if well-managed, make a school highly successful. Spending precious staff meeting time on what kind of paper the art faire entries should be mounted on, is prioritizing the art faire above the instructional business of the school. It is unfair to be frustrated with your staff because they're failing to organize around improving the quality of instruction when you are modeling that what you value above instruction is the students' bathroom behavior.

The difference is what the leader values. It's funny, when you value instruction and prioritize the conversations around that, the plant-management issues tend to be diluted – they are a small piece of the background of the school. They don't go away fully, but they are managed quickly and oftentimes avoided before they even arise. When a leader values plant management or logistics above all else, then the majority of the conversations and meetings are around logistics. So when it comes time to discuss instruction, the logistics-centered school just lacks practice in talking about teaching and they tend to do it less.

Side note: If you are reading this and you think, "Geez, this Jill Jackson is way off base and must not know what real school leadership is all about. The bathroom problems, the bus duty, the coverage for late teachers are major parts of my job every day. Jill needs to get realistic!," then let's step aside for a quick side conversation. I understand that running a big operation from a logistics perspective is tricky and very time-consuming, but I also know that the successful school across town that spends more than eighty percent of their time focusing on instruction-related discussions also has a big operation to run.

It's time to mobilize your leadership team and get them involved in helping you plan staff meetings, team meetings and school-based professional development around what the real needs of the teachers and students are. It's also time to begin to model professional conduct and structure the meetings and interactions of the school around 100 percent teacher engagement, 100 percent teacher focus and 100 percent commitment to moving the focus from what the teachers need to what the students need. These are not student issues – these are teacher issues. And if you fail to intervene and refocus now, you're ensuring full burnout in the very near future.

What Principals with Backbone Know About the Teaching Staff

Let me tell you a little story about a gal with standards. I have a client who just oozes "I am in control"-ness when she enters the room. She is fun, loves to laugh and people clamor to work for her. But boy, she's tough. Her staff of principals will come from other meetings where their thumbs are getting a full text workout on their Blackberries, but when they show up to her meetings, the phones are off and the focus is on the tasks at hand. Yeah, they talk behind her back about how tough-as-nails she is, and how if a phone goes off during her meetings, she asks the person to leave, take the call and talks with them afterward about what they missed while they were out, but they secretly love it.

The reason they love being led with a backbone is because when they're in meetings with her, they get so much done. The meetings are spent mulling over their next steps as a leadership team, getting their hands dirty in the data, determining what the next line of professional development should be, and sharing what's going right with their work. At the end of every meeting, they spend three minutes setting the agenda for the next meeting and turning on their phones and programming the time into their calendars. This is the only time the phones are turned on in the room. She doesn't remind them of the meetings or send four "don't forget" messages. Why should she? They already have it on their calendars and they want to be there because she gets them quickly steeped in the work – they don't waste any time.

She has standards and is unashamed in protecting them. That is her *main job*.

Here's the big take-away from backbone-having leaders: Your staff doesn't set the standards – you do. They don't get to choose whether they meet the standards – you require it. If they aren't meeting your standards – talk to them. If they continue to not meet your standards – write them up.

Now don't get all "we can't fire a teacher because of the union" on me. Can you write up a teacher for not following through on your expectations? Yes you can. When you have a backbone, you care more about protecting the mission to increase achievement than you do having a dust-up with the union. Don't worry about whether you can hire or fire right now – worry about refining professionalism. I guarantee that if you formally write up one teacher for choosing to not meet your standards and expectations, the other few who are doing the same will make a different choice. Notice that I used the word "choice." You have the choice to make the standards and the teachers have the choice to follow them.

Ninety percent or more of your teachers will choose to do the right thing, but it's your dealing with the ten percent who don't that determines whether you have a backbone…and choose to use it.

Leaders with backbone know that in order for their school to have a laser-like focus on instructional improvement, their operating rules have to be tight. I have led hundreds of our clients to create a set of simple non-negotiables – or rules of engagement around the instructional tasks of the school. Some folks shy away from using the term "non-negotiables" and they'd rather call them "agreements" – it doesn't really matter what you call them, as long as you have them.

Here you see a sample of one school's non-negotiables for the implementation of their reading intervention program. This school looked oddly similar to the scene depicted at the beginning of the chapter – they were going through the motions, focused on the problems not the solutions, and were generally spending more time on what concerned the adults rather than dealing with the glaringly obvious instructional needs of the students. The principal was fed up with the constant crabbing about what wasn't working and the excuses about why sixty-eight percent of the student body was performing below benchmark in reading and math. He was so burdened, tired and ready to quit, that he decided he ought to give it one more shot….but this time with backbone.

Evergreen Middle School
Literacy Implementation Non-Negotiables and Agreements

1. We will follow the curriculum map as designed and in its entirety.
2. We agree to create and adhere to the pacing plans for our intervention program. If we anticipate a change in the pacing plan, we will arrive on a solution and plan of action in conjunction with the coach.
3. We will attend and fully participate in all professional development offered to us, and plan with department teammates to implement information learned at professional development.
4. We agree to ask all questions, seek clarification, express concerns and find solutions to the issues or concerns that might inhibit our best teaching of reading.
5. We agree to make significant instructional decisions, alterations and plans in collaboration with our department teammates and site leadership.
6. We agree to follow the meeting procedures during our grade level team meetings. We also agree to implement agreed upon "next steps" immediately following the grade level meetings.
7. We agree to engage in regular coaching with the site instructional coach (pre-conference, observation/demonstration/analysis, debriefing, observing other teachers, hosting teachers in my room) and implement suggestions and new insights
8. We agree to teach each instructional block daily from August 23, 2011 to June 4, 2012.
9. We agree to utilize our SpEd staff and support personnel to provide daily instruction and teaching directly to students during their time in our classrooms.
10. We agree to administer and report the benchmark standards tests according to the curriculum map, and turn the results sheets into the office no later than two days following the assessment date.

Notice in the example above, the non-negotiables detail the principal's and staff's expectation for:

- Using the curricular material adopted by the school
- Analyzing common forms of data
- Participating in and implementing professional development information
- Airing out confusion and frustration productively with colleagues
- Using all of the instructional minutes in the day for the highest level of instruction
- Ensuring that every teacher receives coaching and feedback regardless of expertise and years of experience
- Using the teaming structure to make important instructional decisions and adjustments
- Committing to teaching all of the students all of the standards for the grade level

Well, that just about covers exactly what happens every day in excellent schools with excellent, backboned leaders! They leverage non-negotiables to set the stage for the high-level instructional work that needs to be done.

Side note: You don't want to make this mistake that I've seen non-backboned, weak principals make about non-negotiables. I worked with one principal who very weakly photocopied a sample list of non-negotiables that I had given her as a sample during a training and attached a note to teachers that said, "Sign this so that I know that you understand the expectations." Then, she dropped it into their boxes one night when everyone had gone home. The next afternoon, she received three complaints from the Union because they thought the non-negotiables were an addendum to the contract!

Um, how do I put this nicely. Non-backbone principal alert! The purpose of the non-negotiables is to work <u>with</u> your staff and <u>alongside</u> each other to create a joint set of expectations of what needs to happen daily in order to raise the overall quality of the teaching. It's the staff and principal's job to identify non-negotiables. It's the principal's job to ensure that everyone is following them.

The goal of setting non-negotiables is to organize the conversations, activities and decisions upon the base of great professional conduct. For example, backboned leaders don't spend time negotiating whether the assessment results need to be entered into the program on time. They've set that as a baseline expectation and they have it on their secretary's calendar to make sure that it has been done. If the secretary has found that two teachers haven't put their scores in the system by the designated time, they call the teacher and let them know that the scores need to be entered by the end of the school day so that she can print the reports for the principal. If it happens more than twice, the secretary lets the principal know and the principal calls the teacher in. The principal lets the teacher know that if he or she fails to enter the scores on time, then she will be forced to put a formal letter in the teacher's file.

Is this harsh? To some, but so are the results from spending time on no-return type tasks.

When leaders have a backbone, they don't waste their time following up on baseline tasks that are expected of everyone. They spend their time on real instructional leadership tasks like pouring over the school data and meeting with teacher teams to discuss progress and next steps. Whether you waste your time or spend your time improving the quality of instruction is your choice. You set the tone and you either expect it or you don't.

Notice, however, that the non-negotiables are not a set of "rules for teachers" – professional dress code, showing up on time to school, supervision duties and tasks related to logistics management are not addressed here. In fact, if you have those types of concerns at your school, you probably need a lot more than a set of non-negotiables. The professional conduct expectations that answer this question – "What does it look like when we're busy improving the quality of instruction?" – are what is really important. The cool thing? *Your non-negotiables, when clearly outlined, expected and enforced, will simply become how your school does business every day.*

You will see the effect of your non-negotiables in your student achievement and your staff morale.

So This Is What a Backbone-Having Conversation Sounds Like:

"Staff, I am coming to you today with some information that is very important and that we will revisit over the next month. I need your full attention, as what I will share with you will become your responsibility to carry out.

I have noticed that we are spending an inordinate amount of time during staff meetings, team meetings and one-on-ones talking about what is not working, how we don't have enough time to do our jobs, and how some folks on our staff are not pulling their weight. I agree that these things are issues and it's my expectation that over the next trimester we will work to move from focusing on what is not working to what is working.

This focus on what is not working has resulted in a very staff-centered attitude, rather than a student and data-centered mindset. Our students' learning has suffered because of it. And, for the fourth year in a row, we are on the district's neediest school list. What I notice is that we spend much of our collaboration time making decisions about what is convenient for us. We are failing to focus on what our students need and orienting our discussions toward that. I hold myself responsible for not addressing this sooner, as this has been an ongoing struggle at our school.

Specifically, I will be working through a process with you to create a set of what we'll call Non-Negotiables for Excellent Teaching. These are not rules, they are expectations for professional actions that every staff member will be held accountable for creating and adhering to. I am working on how I will hold everyone, including myself, accountable to embracing and adhering to these Non-Negotiables. These agreements will help us shape the culture of our school, one conversation at a time. I will need your full participation and commitment and am expecting just that from every one of you. When we analyze why some schools in our district are very successful and others, like us, aren't, much of it comes down to the staff taking their professional responsibilities very seriously.

Excellent schools are made up of regular educators who <u>choose</u> to do business differently. I am choosing to do business differently and focus on what we have control over, not those things that are out of our control. We have everything we need to get the job done and teach in ways that get our students to work at unprecedented levels. We are a very skilled staff with so much to offer our students and I look forward to structuring how we improve the quality of instruction together in this school year together. I appreciate your commitment to improving our school and would welcome any feedback and questions about our upcoming work in this area.

At our next meeting, we will work together to define the Non-Negotiables for professional collaboration. The meeting after that, we will develop the Non-Negotiables about instructional planning and assessment. Come prepared with ideas and questions – I will structure our meetings to ensure that we have 100 percent involvement from our staff."

Planning for *Your* Backbone-Having Conversation:

Question 1: *Have you clearly outlined non-negotiables for your system? What are they?*

_____

_____

Question 2: *How did you communicate them?*

_____

_____

Question 3: *What currently exists to hold personnel accountable for following the non-negotiables?*

_____

_____

Question 4: *How do you measure whether the non-negotiables are followed?*

_____

_____

Question 5: *How do you refer to and review the non-negotiables? How often?*

_____

_____

Question 6: *If you could revise what you have in place, what revisions would you make?*

_____

_____

Accountability in Schools: Purpose Driven or Fear Driven?

Originally published on www.jackson-consulting.com
on November 26, 2012

I often wonder if we changed our thinking about accountability in schools, if we'd get a better result in the classrooms?

Here's what I'm thinking: **Instead of focusing on** *accountability* **(of tests, of standards, of evaluations, of observations) we should focus on** *responsibility* **and create** *purpose*.

In fact, accountability in schools can just feel like "Big Brother's watching over my shoulder" when it's not attached to *responsibility and purpose*. Think about it, when we just go about our business and we're focused on "meeting the expectations of 'the district,' " there is little oomph (or joy!) in the work. But when I'm really super excited and invested in a particular subject area or technique I'm using with my kids, I'm teaching like my hair's on fire – accountability or no accountability!

Here's the deal, accountability in schools is a given – we don't have a choice. But purpose? Well, we have a *big opportunity to* create, recreate and be motivated by purpose every day. And that's no one's job but our own!

Let's look at a good working definition of accountability: the state of being accountable, liable, or answerable.

Now let's take a look at a definition of purpose:

1. *the reason for which something exists or is done, made, used, etc.*
2. *an intended or desired result; end; aim; goal.*
3. *determination; resoluteness.*

Hmmm….

Here's what popped out to me as I read those definitions: **Purpose is not just a "pie-in-the-sky" idea or thought – it's built upon action and *results*. And accountability is *results* driven, too!**

Soooo…without purpose, accountability is *always* going to feel like "the district" or "the man" is breathing down our necks!

Let me tell you a little story that just happened THIS MORNING!

We work with some larger school districts with the goal of helping them implement their reading programs and get organized on their Common Core implementations. One of our districts has nineteen elementary schools – **they're all trying to accomplish the *same thing* and they are held accountable for the same levels of performance**: implement their reading programs so expertly that they get 80 percent or more kids on benchmark just with their Tier I instruction! (By the way, it IS possible…email me if you want to know how!)

I had two emails from this particular client in my inbox this morning: One email from what I consider to be an "on fire" principal – SHE ISN'T MESSING AROUND! (My kind of gal.) She was **asking for some feedback on a letter that she was sending her staff, motivating them to really power through until the holidays,** rather than limp into the holidays – she was having them choose two kids in their classrooms that are not currently benchmark, but would be by December 15th.

And then one email from a very nice, kind principal complaining that he just "doesn't have any time to get into classrooms because **he spends his time putting out fires all day" and he's behind on his observations and hasn't met with his leadership team** lately.

Well, I have news for ya: both principals have the same size schools, the same highly impacted, low poverty clientele and are held to the same standards…as they should be! **One is getting it done and asking the district to come walk through the classrooms, and the other is mulling over the same stuff as last year and is bemoaning why "the district" always shows up unannounced** to walk through classrooms.

What's the difference? Not accountability! They both have visits from the district.

The difference is *purpose linked to accountability.* The principal who asked for feedback from me on her mission for her teachers is doing what she's doing because she's passionate about the "doing" for their students. She's not worrying at all about "the district" or "the test." The other principal? He's so focused on "the district" and "the test" that he's, *at best,* trying to meet the minimum requirement.

Doesn't sound very inspiring to me...what do YOU think?

BUT HERE'S THE DEAL! **Accountability is what "they" put into place to monitor school improvement, but meaning and purpose is what "we" put into place to drive us each day** – - especially on those days when we don't have accountability checks.

It's like exercise, guys. Do I get up and do my exercising when my exercising partner is sick and doesn't show up on my back door at 5:30 a.m.? Or do I snooze and decide to sleep in? If I snooze and sleep in then I'm accountability driven – motivated only by my friend showing up on my back doorstep. If I get my tired and lazy behind up, then I'm purpose driven – I know that I am committed to improving my health even on those days I don't feel like it.

5
The Teaching Teams

"Backbone beats wishbone every time."
– Unknown

The Scene: You walk into Room 10 at 10:45 to join the 7th grade team meeting that takes place during their 10:00 a.m. prep period and there's no one there. So you go into Rooms 11 and 12 to find the team, but it's not until you get to Room 16 that you find Mrs. Harmon and she reports that the team got done early with the meeting and so they headed back to their rooms at about 10:30. You ask her what actions they decided to take at the end of the meeting, based upon the CRT data they were supposed to look at today in their meeting and she says, "We talked about some ideas for teaching vocabulary a bit differently and maybe adding in some small group teaching but we really didn't decide anything. Most of us agreed that we could start that next semester."

As you head back to your office a little perturbed, you stop by the staff lounge and you find the other seventh grade team members drinking their coffee and looking through pictures of a recently married colleague. You ask them, "So guys, what did you decide to do about the CRT data?" They kind of look at each other and then Ms.

Samuelson says, "We really didn't decide anything, but here's our meeting record sheet." When you take the meeting record sheet back to your office you realize that they've "filled out" the sheet but it's hardly complete. And when you recognize that they nowhere on the sheet did it mention anything about vocabulary or small groups. It is mostly blank.

The Analysis: You have not successfully outlined a common task for your teachers to work on and without it, there is no purpose. When you go back and review your team record sheets from the past few months, you notice that teachers have not really done anything that has impact on the quality of instruction. A They are "meeting to meet" – and doing it poorly at that! They are unclear as to what they were supposed to accomplish or even if there was a purpose for the meeting, other than the fact that it was on the schedule. The teachers obviously do not have a problem meeting (they *are* meeting around the colleague's wedding picture), but they lack purpose. If vocabulary and small groups are not part of your instructional goal then even if they are talking about instruction, it might be so random and disconnected from the school goals that is has little value.

No one is taking responsibility for the grade level work and there is no plan to *do* anything following the meeting. Without action or movement, the meeting is useless and there is no impact on the quality of instruction.

As the leader, you have to come to terms with this fact: *If you don't like the behaviors that you're seeing in your staff as a whole, you have to stop those behaviors and replace them with something else.*

What Principals with Backbone Know About the Teaching Teams

Here's a little side story that has really helped me figure out how to energize and mobilize teaching teams: When I was a teacher, we used to have a Breakfast with Santa pancake fest every holiday season. It was fun because we got to flip pancakes and sausages and hang out with the families and other staff members in a casual environment. Oh, and we also got to perfect our Mickey Mouse pancakes, which was a skill that has served me well in life! Most of the staff came to flip pancakes, take tickets, be the shopkeeper at Santa's Store or generally harass the other teachers while they worked. We had a great staff, but there were folks that worked really hard, folks who were there for the fun, folks who were there for the pancakes, and folks who spent their time dodging their jobs. But when the last pancake was flipped and the holiday tunes were played out, it was time to clean up. *Everyone* (and I really mean everyone) helped to wipe the tables down, fold them up, bag the trashcans, clean the griddles, put the speaker system away, sweep the floor, take down the decorations and pick up trash. Did we like it? Not necessarily. Was it the way we wanted to spend a Saturday morning? Probably not.

But we did it. Why? Because we had a common task at hand: clean up. The interesting part is that when folks would show up on the scene during clean-up, they would just pitch in even though they weren't asked to. A common task draws people in.

My point is this: even tasks that we really don't want to do will get done, if the backbone-enforced principal sets the expectation and the task.

Let's go back to the 7th grade team described at the start of the chapter for a minute. They knew they had to meet, so they did. If we had interviewed the principal, she would have let us know that, indeed, that *was* the task and that *was* the expectation: to meet. Yes, there was data to look at, but just looking at the data isn't really a task – it's what you want folks to *do* with the data as they look at it that defines the task.

The missing piece was a task linked to action. By prescribing carefully orchestrated tasks (that are linked to your instructional goals) and then holding folks accountable to carrying out these tasks according to your expectations, you are *training your staff how to be professionals.*

We can assume that the principal did want them to do something with the data, but without defining what that was, the teachers probably looked at the data and made a few comments and moved on. They needed the structure and guidelines that come with creating an agenda with a purpose. If I were to revamp that 7th grade meeting, I would ask myself these questions in preparation:

1. What instructional goal do I want the teachers to focus on as they review the data? What questions will I provide them so they get to the heart of the data?

2. What trends in the data have I noticed that I want them to pay particular attention to?

3. How will I know that they have analyzed the data? What is the "product" I want to see?

4. What are sample next steps I could provide to support them in determining the actions that they'll take?

5. How long do I imagine this analysis of the data/common task will take to complete?

6. If they feel like they're "done early," how can I help shape a secondary task so that they don't walk away from the valuable collaboration time?

In fact, I typically use a template such as the one below to help them capture the important information and structure the meeting so that it's of value as we carry out our mission. The form is not a log of what we have done, it is a Plan of Action of what we will do – a commitment to *doing something* more than just meeting. In fact, the meeting is just the starting point for something to come – the place the ideas are birthed.

Super Simple Grade Level Meeting Plan of Action

Notetaker: _____
The notetaker takes notes on pertinent information of the conversation and will confirm with teammates what will be written down so that it represents the entire team's information and views.

Facilitator: _____
Facilitator keeps the conversation moving, insures that one person does not dominate the conversation and that everyone shares their ideas and responses. Facilitator returns the grade level meeting form to principal and places a copy of the team meeting notes in Assistant Principal and grade level teams' mailboxes.

Timekeeper: _____
Timekeeper monitors the amount of time spent on each task and makes the team aware of their need to move past a particular subject or topic, if the conversation is stalling.

*Roles will rotate each week

Date: _____
Time in: _____ **Time out:** _____

Your Team's Meeting Goal:
To analyze the CRT data and make two (2) daily instructional adjustments in every classroom that take into account the data you've reviewed.

Looking at the data (5 minutes):
- Which students have made gains, according to their CRT data? What do we attribute these gains to?
- Which students are receiving intervention (Tier II or III) and is it working? How do we know?
- What kind of instruction is being provided for Tier II students by the classrooms teachers? Do we have evidence that it's working fast enough and at the rates that we'd expect from solid Tier II instruction?
- Which areas do we need to know more about? What will give us this information?

Common Task to Complete + Product (10 minutes):
Your job is to create a two-column chart that shows which students (by name and class) met proficiency level on the CRT. Then highlight in yellow the students below proficiency who are receiving secondary services and highlight the students in pink who are below proficiency and not receiving secondary services.

Then, jointly write five statements about your deconstructed data. These statements will become your "to solve" discussion points in next week's team meeting, where the Interventionists and Special Ed teacher will be present.

Action Steps/Who Will Do What/By When (5 minutes):

Planning for next meeting (5 minutes):
List your five statements of fact about the data

1.

2.

3.

4.

5.

A motivated, driven kind of leader sits down with the instructional coach and combs through the grade level reports weekly, noting where the coach can provide support to the teams and specific teachers. The coach and principal also assess the quality of the work that was done during the team meeting:

- Was it connected to the goals?
- Was it completed with care?
- Are the next-steps realistic and doable in the amount of time listed?
- Are they high-impact tasks that are worthy of the team's time or is there a need for adjustment?
- Are the same people doing all of the work or is the work spread equally across the team?
- Is this in line with the work from other teams?
- How does this impact my plan for the next team meeting? Do we need to adjust?
- Has this team identified ideas that the coach and I need to share with other teacher teams?
- Is the structure of the team meeting still suiting our needs?
- Is the form that we use still suiting our needs?

Side note: As I was writing this chapter, I avoided using the term "establish norms" on purpose. I find that the groups that are obsessed about "reviewing norms" ad nauseum are usually the groups who have none. They use the "reviewing of norms" as a crutch to deal with un-professional behaviors that interrupt the work of the team. I recently worked with a group that reviewed norms at the beginning of each meeting. While the norms were read by one person, the group trickled in. They were breaking the norms while the norms were being read!

So the takeaway on norms is that, yes, norms are great. Yes, you need to have a baseline of behaviors that needs to be present every time a group meets in a school. But if you're whipping people with the norms, then you probably have some leadership work to do around backbone, not norms. Just like we have to teach, model, practice and apply new concepts to our students, backbone-having leaders do not assume that their staff knows how to act and do during team meetings – they teach them how. Norms are a tool for teaching, but in no way take the place of backbone!

So the key is this:

Regular meeting schedule/regular meeting organization

+

**Meaningful tasks/discussions/
"doing" kind of work around your instruction goals**

=

Successful teaming

Side note: Notice how this chapter relies heavily on you having a fully-developed, expertly implemented set of non-negotiables? If you can't get people to meetings on time, there is no way the high level questions above are going to be thoughtfully answered. If some folks stonewall and won't participate because they're mad and pouting at other team members, there is no way you will collectively complete and master your school goals. The non-negotiables support the quality of the work that needs to be carried out and become increasingly central to your school's success.

So This Is What a Backbone-Having Conversation Sounds Like with the Team

"Hi team! I want to follow up with you on last meeting's team report. I noticed that your team (and several others) is not using the full team meeting time for goal-related work and that you're often ending early. I also noticed that most of the "to do" items that you reported were things for the Special Ed team to work on, and that on the last team meeting notes, there were no 'next steps' that everyone on your team is carrying out. I got to thinking that we need to look at our meeting structure and our meeting results and make sure that we're using that time to help our teams collectively meet our school's instructional goals.

I'd like to start with our team agenda. I usually set the basic focus for your team meeting and the nitty gritty is left to your teams. Are you finding that you need more input or guidance as you discuss or work on the meeting focus? Would it help your team if I provided several guiding questions related to the meeting focus to get your conversation jump-started and on the right track? At what point do you typically "run out of things to talk about" during your meetings?

These ideas are great! I'll start to give you 3-4 guiding questions that relate back to the focus area. I would like to see your teammates each take responsibility for participating in the conversation – let's talk about how to structure this the next time we meet. Also, I really like the idea of keeping a running question list for the coach and me – what if we made another column on our agenda that would be a spot for you to pose questions to us? That will signal that we need to get back to you within 48 hours of your meeting with answers/information/clarification and help you continue to build your team momentum.

The other important idea that I want to work on with you is developing a common task for each grade level teaming meeting. I find that when I pop into meetings, oftentimes the same people are doing most of the talking and non-talking and sometimes the conversation can get stale. I have contrasted those conversations with the lively, engaged discussions we have when we read, chart and discuss articles at our staff meetings. I realize that we need to structure our team meetings much like we do our staff meeting so that we get the same result. I want to us to commit to developing short- and long-term tasks that we work on – and that actually have a product. I'll bet we will have even better engagement and conversation when we really get in there and get our hands dirty. We need to get beyond 'just talking.'

What do you think about a common task? Do you think it's a huge stretch for your team? Can you think of a common task that we could add in to our next team meeting – a task that will help us improve the quality of our instruction? The one thing that comes to mind right away is creating a checklist based upon our last PD day at the district. Remember the presenter gave us those slides with '10 Steps for Boosting Vocabulary Instruction in the Content Areas?' I overhead Don and Trisha say that they would love to have those 10 Steps on a checklist for their preparation…and that does connect with our school goal of adding in pre-teaching vocabulary to our ELL students. Would that be a valuable task for your team to work on during your next team meeting? Think about it and let me know by Tuesday afternoon so that I can help you craft the next agenda.

I am really excited about investigating ways that we can use our teaming time more effectively. As I leave now, I would like your team to spend 5 minutes brainstorming ways that you can make your team meetings more efficient and effective. Cedric – would you bring me that list when you're done?"

Planning for *Your* Backbone-Having Conversation:

Question #1: *Are teams meeting for a purpose or are we meeting just to meet? Have I made the teams' main focus to work on the instructional goals or is that just implied?*

_____

_____

Question #2: *Are teams re-hashing old issues or unsolvable issues, or are we focusing on what we actually have control over?*

_____

_____

Question #3: *Do teams name students <u>by name</u> when we talk, or do we talk in generalities?*

_____

_____

Question #4: *Do teams have a running list of what we've tried and what happened, or do we approach each meeting like we've never seen each other before?*

_____

_____

Question #5: *Do teams leave each meeting with something instructional to do, or are we focused mainly on non-instructional tasks?*

_____

_____

Question #6: *Which team has the most developed team meetings? Could they model their meetings for the other teams to see? Who are my power-team members that I can tap into?*

_____

_____

Urgent: The Dr.'s Prescription for Your "It Would Be Nice If"- Syndrome

Originally published on www.jackson-consulting.com
on September 17, 2012

We're suffering. From something that's totally treatable. But we have to act fast.

What ails us?

It's the "It would be nice if"- syndrome.

Here's what it sounds like:

- It would be nice if I had more prep time
- It would be nice if the grade level before us would actually teach the kids what they need to know for my grade level
- It would be nice if the kids would actually do their homework
- It would be nice if I could have more aide time
- It would be nice if we didn't have to have all those walk-throughs during my teaching

Here's the problem with the "It would be nice if"- syndrome:

- It's built around talking – not action. And successful schools are all about the doing, not just the chatting.
- It's focusing on a dream world. I hate to break it to you, but we work with kids. Kids do not exist in a dream world…they pull us right into reality. Every day.
- It takes the focus off of what matters most: the quality of the interaction between the teacher and the students.
- It kills our momentum. We lose ground when we waste our time talking about things that might not happen – plus we give away our instructional power when we base our students' success on external sources.

So….you might be wondering what the heck you *do* about the "It would be nice if"- syndrome. Well, Dr. Jackson, (I'm not really a doctor, but I play one in this blog) has just the prescription for you!

Prescription One: Realize right now that the return on your teaching begins with the *prep*. If you have a highly prepped lesson, you have less behavioral interruptions, more engagement and have more time during the lesson to listen to your students and see what their learning.

Prescription Two: When you are in teacher meetings/team meetings, focus the work on *tasks*, not just discussions. If you find that your team is all talk/no action, throw in one of these statements: "Ok guys. Let's talk about what we're going to *do* after this conversation," or "Alrighty. Let's focus on what we have control of so that we can get started right away." Focusing on an action immediately pulls you out of the all talk/no action problem. Sometimes we're just in a bad habit of doing way more talking than we do acting and we just need someone to help us get pulled out of it. Let that person be *you*!

Prescription Three: Analyze your time spent at work. How much time is spent talking about the heart of instruction? How much time is spent actually crafting lessons and not just prepping materials? How much reflective conversation do you have with your coaches or your colleagues about your teaching? These types of questions drive your time and conversations directly back to that interaction between teacher and student – and that's what really matters!

If you suffer from the "It would be nice if"- syndrome, then it's your responsibility to take steps to recover. Here's the cool thing: It's actually pretty simple to recover. You start by doing.

Yep, that's it!

6
The Most Resistant Teacher

"The individual activity of one man with backbone will do more than a thousand men with a mere wishbone."
– William J. H. Boetcker

The Scene: You are experiencing a high level of reluctance from the 1st grade team. The team leader, Ronald, has been resistant from the start of the school year, rarely attends grade level meetings, tries to coax the other team members into not sharing their assessment data or bringing necessary materials, and has, from time to time, locked his door during reading instruction to deny entry during observations. You've noticed that grade level teachers who were onboard at the beginning of the school year are starting to keep their distance, and adopting a "these kids will never learn" attitude shared by the team leader. In front of you, Ronald talks a good game and even requests the coach's support, but when you attempt to follow up, he puts off scheduling anything with the coach. Recently, you walked up to Ronald and a group talking in the staff lounge and overhead him questioning your leadership ability and the direction you're taking the school. His wife is the union President.

The Analysis: You've got more than one problem to work through – all of which are going to require some serious "backbone-ish-ness." (Yes, I just made that up) The first problem is that Ronald has been disrespecting the Non-Negotiables by not coming to meetings at all, and when he does, he's unprepared. How long has this been going on? My instinct is that Ronald has been allowed to do his own thing with little, if any, consequence for quite awhile. Just like it has taken time for Ronald to get to this point of resistance, it's going to take skill and stamina on your part to fix it in the short- and long-term. The other glaring issue is that Ronald is affecting his team – and you can't afford for the whole team to turn to the negative side. Begin by approaching individual teammates of Ronald's for check-ins. Be pleasant, but be visible. Ask a member or two of the 1st grade team to join the Leadership Team and begin to expose them to other positive, forward-thinkers on the staff. This will dilute the effect that Ronald has had on the team.

You must have a very direct discussion with Ronald about the conversation you overhead him having with his colleagues. It's important to tip Ronald off that you know what is going on and to give him an opportunity to talk about it. Something as simple as, "Hey Ronald – as I was walking in the hallway on Tuesday, I overheard you sharing with Mrs. Goble that you didn't feel confident about the direction that we're taking the school. Let's talk about that – do you have a second or would 3:30 p.m. work?" Keep the conversation to "we", not "I". You do not want to go to battle with Ronald, you simply want to put him on notice that you recognize that he is struggling to follow through on the Non-Negotiables and working to meet the school's instructional goal.

Side note: Even if Ronald is a teacher that gets great results from his students each year, this conversation is a "must" for you, principal. Ronald's ability to partner with his teammates to discuss student results, implement professional development and genuinely transform his classroom according to the instructional goal is essential to the success of his students, his team and your school. This is not a conversation about results of the students, this is a conversation about results of the teacher.

What Principals with Backbone Know About the Most Resistant Teacher:

I find myself saying this to struggling principals continually: *You take care of your great teachers by taking care of your resistant ones.*

It's really true. There is no way to burn out a great or promising teacher faster than teaming him up with a resistant, crabby, "nothing's-gonna-work-around-this-dump-of-a-school" kind of teammate.

When I was a teacher, I was paired up with two teachers who had taught for awhile together – they had quite a few years of teaching under their belts. As a teacher moving from primary grades to intermediate, I was really excited about the new challenge and couldn't wait to learn the new curriculum (I'm kind of a teaching-nerd like that!) and figure out what "big kids" could do. I was used to the little guys and gals that came in not knowing how to line up – let alone knowing their math facts. What you need to know about me is that I am really enthusiastic about things related to teaching – I love teaching. I still am excited and energized by the possibilities we have before us in schools, so I had a pretty strong "let's do this!" attitude when I joined this new team.

I spent the summer getting ready for the big bad upper grades – and I couldn't wait. I set my room up in a new way, tried some new bulletin board configurations, had my students' folders all organized and then spent the first week of school with the kids getting the room all spiffed up with our work, so that as parents came to the class for Back to School Night they knew we were already getting down to business.

Well, on the day before Back to School night, my team teachers and I met for our grade level meeting in my classroom. Incidentally, it was the first time that my teammates had come to visit my room. (*Big red flag!* I was a little dense). The first thing out of one teacher's mouth when she walked in the door was, "Oh what – are you trying to show us up?" I remember thinking when I went into their rooms, "Geez, I wonder when they're going to start decorating for the beginning of school?" (They never did). But I was shocked that she was literally *angry* with me because I had gone above the norm. I brushed it off and kept doing my thing, but I remember that I felt almost embarrassed about doing "too much" in her eyes.

As the Fall went on, we ate lunch together, we did car duty together and generally were attached at each other's hips throughout the day – by necessity, but joined-at-the-hip nonetheless. One day my principal whispered to me during lunch, "Can you come in my office? We need to chat." After nearly *dying* inside, I went in and sat down. And here was the conversation:

Principal: *"I want to talk to you about how your attitude has grown increasingly negative this year."*

Me: (Practically choking) *"Oh my gosh, what do you mean?"*

Principal: *"You were always the kind of teacher who burst through the door of the office with a funny story to tell about your kids or the latest update on who scored well on the latest assessment. You don't do that anymore. I see you rolling your eyes about what your kids have done. I hear you entering into conversations with your teammates about how your kids didn't do things the ways you wanted them to. Do you recognize any of this?"*

Me: (Holding back tears) *"I had no idea! I will fix it immediately because I don't want to be like that! I'm so sorry!"*

Principal: *"I wanted to bring it to your attention so that you can be aware of the tone and the way you're talking with your teammates about the students. I know you'll make the change and this is not who you are."*

Me: (Practically having a mental breakdown at this point) *"Thank you. I will."*

That was one of the most excruciating conversations that I've had with someone, but also one I'm most grateful for and here's why: I would characterize myself as very high on an enthusiastic and positive thinking scale and I thought that no one could alter that. But what I realized is that even the most positive go-getter, if exposed to negativity and resistance, is susceptible to falling into resistance and negativity. Believe me, if I can, anyone can.

Backboned principals ask me, "So, how do I reward the teachers who are doing the right things?"

My answer: Take care of the ones who aren't.

Side note: The funny thing about resistance is if you were to poll your staff anonymously and had them report who the three most resistant staff members are, I'll bet you at least 90 percent of the time they'd list the same three people. Everyone knows. And principals with a backbone know that the second they have a backbone-havin' conversation with the most resistant teacher, <u>everyone</u> in the school will hear about it. The funny thing to me is that when the biggest resistor is telling everyone how "mean" and "unfair" you are, most of the folks will nod and say, "Oh yes, I understand" to their faces, but behind the scenes? They're fist pumping and calling each other on the sly and saying, "Finally!" And the best by-product of taking care of the biggest resistor? You restore your staff's faith in your ability to protect them from whatever gets in the way of improving the quality of their teaching.

Principals with a backbone know that *resistance comes in many forms and they know how to spot it from a mile away.* Resistors come in many shapes, sizes and masks. My personal favorite is the "I-Don't-Like-What-You're-Saying Eye-Contact-Avoider." When I am doing coaching work in a school or district, I am typically there to solve problems – 100 percent of the time people need to improve their scores and I'm there to help them deal with the cold, hard facts. I've gotten pretty good an sizing people up quickly – this helps me tailor my approach to how the room feels and reads. When I have a teacher, coach, principal or district leader who won't make eye contact, I know *right away* that we've got some resistance going on. So, what I'll typically do is slip in a question to that person like, "Jonah, tell me what's cropping up for you about this right now."

Well, Mr. No-Eye-Contact Jonah will typically avert his eyes (even though I'm staring right at him) and say really quickly, "Nothing. Everything's fine." Then he quickly goes back to sustained, silent staring. I've also run into resistors that use crying (This is my second personal favorite resisting strategy!) as a method to keep me off track. Every time we talk about making a change that will require a lot of work, or are addressing some pretty negative student data, this person will just start tearing up and working herself (sorry ladies, it's typically a woman) into a full-blown cry. It's funny, I remember that when I was having a fairly tough data conversation with a struggling teacher alongside the principal, the teacher started crying and finally said, "I'm sorry, I'm just so unfocused. I'm going through a divorce and it's just so hard!" I am tough, but I have a heart! So, I said to the teacher, "How about we take a break for today and I'll meet with you in the morning." When she left, I said to the principal, "That's too bad to hear that she's going through a divorce – that's tough." The principal laughed at me and said, "She went through a divorce *eleven years ago!*

Oops!

Whether it's the over-talker, the behind-the-back whisperer, the constant avoider, the parking lot gossip monger, or the "that's not how our old principal did it" resistor, you've got to deal with the resistance before it infects your staff. Resistance is like a virus – the longer it exists, the stronger it gets.

Principals with a backbone know that *resistance happens when changes loom*. I'm fascinated by my finding that folks are resistant for one of two main issues: they don't have the skill to carry out what you're asking them to do or they are willfully working against your change efforts. I call this "the case of skill or will." While the resistance might *look* the same, the root cause could be radically different. If you know that folks are resistant because they just don't know *how* to do what you want them to do, for gosh sakes, get them some coaching help! Their resistance comes from feelings of inadequacy. At this point, strategically backboned principals will weave in peer coaching or your instructional coach to support – and you can watch the resistance fade. For the willfully-working-against-the-goals folks, you've got to take control of them – they are your job. And the conversation coming later in this chapter is for you.

Principals with a backbone know that *anything beyond short-term resistance is contagious*. Look, you can't start confronting everyone who shows signs of frustration or anyone who might initially disagree with what you're asking them to do. Some push-back is natural. Push-back and initial resistance keep you honest. In fact, if I know I'm working with a particularly resistant staff, I am better prepared and I do my legwork and research to see all angles. Your naysayers help sharpen you and sharpen your focus. This is where your Leadership Team is invaluable to you. Use them to vet ideas, create new ideas, and even shoot your latest, greatest idea down before you bring it to the entire staff! This is what backboned principals do – they "float" ideas to their leadership team and retool the idea based upon the feedback. I find myself thinking, "Whew! Thank goodness I didn't share that with the entire staff – I would've blown it!" And I have the Leadership Team to thank for that.

Principals can avoid frustration turning into full-blown resistance by dealing directly with it. Something as simple as, "Guys, I know you are really frustrated with the amount of work you're putting into getting your Common Core lessons together. I want you to know that I'm taking our staff meeting time this week and cutting it in half so that you can use the rest of the time to prep your lessons with your team." See? It's simple. It's *communication*.

Side note: I want you to pay attention to how you're talking with your other principal colleagues about your staff. I find that folks are often saying, "Oh my gosh, my staff is soooo not going to like this – they're going to freak out!" When in reality it's just a couple of teachers who are resistant to implementing what it takes to meet your instructional goals. So avoid over-generalizing the resistance and obsessing over the chosen crabby ones. When you really evaluate it, the resistance only sits with one or two people or grade levels. You've got more folks with you than against you, so take care of the ones who are ready for the mission.

This Is What a Backbone-Having Conversation Sounds Like:

Tabatha, I brought you in today to resolve the ongoing problem with your refusal to engage in work with our instructional coach. After this meeting, I expect that you will begin to work with the coach, accepting feedback and implementing the suggestions and support. I have this same expectation of our entire staff. I will ask for your response following the information that I share with you.

I have witnessed you laughing and snickering during the presentations that our instructional coach has given during staff meetings and have witnessed you being intentionally difficult and contrary as the coach works with your team, as well as defiant when she respectfully asks you to try a technique to increase the effectiveness of your teaching. I have seen no evidence that you have followed through on any of the recommendations of the coach.

You must know that the coach's work is directed by me and my desires for our staff, so by failing to implement her support, you are directly defying my expectations of you. You know, Tabatha, that this is not the first time that we have discussed this and I have become increasingly frustrated by your refusal to comply.

I have seen that your lack of follow-through and poor professional conduct has caused you to have a very negative attitude toward your teammates, our school and our district. This has affected your positive attitude with your students and I recognize almost daily that you are very short and impatient with our students. Your attitude is affecting your team, as several people have come to me concerned about working with you next year, due to your negativity.

I realize that I should have come to you sooner to address these issues, as they are a true problem in your classroom, your team and our school. I give you my word that, I will speak with you sooner in the future, if necessary, to allow you to improve your behaviors and responses so that this does not get to this point again.

Tabatha, I am asking you to completely cease mocking the coaching role and to comply with my expectation that every teacher willingly work with the coach on an ongoing basis. If you choose to continue this behavior, your choice will force me to start you on an improvement plan that, if carried out to the fullest, will result in you losing your job.

My desire is to resolve this issue immediately so that we can restore our focus on the instruction of our students. I know that you can do this and I am willing to support you in any way that is appropriate to help you remedy these problems.

Tabatha, I would like to hear your responses to what I have outlined here.

And, just because these conversations are the toughest of all, here's another example:

Charlotte, I've asked to meet with you about the fact that you've chosen not participate in your team meetings for the past month. One of our school's agreements is that each teacher will not only attend the team meetings, but participate and contribute, and your choice to not do so is in direct opposition of what we all agreed were important elements of us working as a team.

Your lack of participation deeply concerns me and has caused me to question your commitment to our school's improvement process. You are directly impacting our student teachers, and your team's less-tenured teachers and their understanding of the importance of teamwork, sharing ideas and working through roadblocks, collectively. It is also imperative that you rely and call upon the expertise of your teammates to help problem solve and plan for instruction for your students, as you do share groups with the other team members. Your lack of participation has direct influence on the quality of instruction that you and your teammates provide to the students in your grade level.

Charlotte, when we are finished with our conversation today, I want us both to leave confidently knowing that we will not have to discuss this problem again. Charlotte, do you have any questions about our conversation?

Tip: Visit Resources 6, 7 and 8 in the Resources section

Planning for *Your* Backbone-Having Conversation:

Question 1: *Who are my top three long-term resistors and what hard evidence do I have that illustrates their resistance?*

_____

_____

Question 2: *Who are my top three short-term resistors that need to become a top priority? Who can I bring in to buddy up with this teacher as we move beyond the resistance?*

_____

_____

Question 3: *What part of the conversation with my resistors will be toughest for me?*

_____

_____

Question 4: *Who can I trust to help me rehearse the conversation with? What kind of feedback do I want?*

_____

_____

Question 5: *What is my biggest source of resistance? Is this related to my instructional goals for the school?*

_____

_____

Question 6: *How can I weave my Leadership Team into the management of resistance in our school? What information do I need from them as I manage and avoid resistance?*

_____

_____

"We'll Do Anything for the Kids" and Other Half-Truths We Tell Ourselves

Originally published on www.jackson-consulting.com
on August 23, 2012

So I'm a little frustrated and here's why…

We're doing our data review and we look at the data from all of our clients and friends and see where they are, what they did, and where they need to head next year with us.

There's some really awesome stuff (take a look at our "Results" tab and you'll get excited!). There's some good stuff. Then there's some frustrating stuff.

What's got me frustrated?

We have worked with a few districts/schools who continue to perform poorly. The fact that they're performing poorly is a problem, of course, and we're working on that.

But the real problem is this: they don't act like they're performing poorly.

What I'm hearing is, **"You know, we're doing it all for the kids."** But what I'm seeing is resistance to guidance.

What I'm hearing is, **"We're doing better than we ever have."** But what I'm seeing are more and more kids ending up in interventions.

What I'm hearing is, **"We are open for feedback."** But when I come back after a few weeks to check on progress, it's like they never heard the feedback and the old practices are firmly in place.

So what gives?

I know that **improving student scores is a very complex task**. I know it's hard. I know it's painful. I know sometimes there's so much work to be done we don't even know where to start! **But we have to stop fooling ourselves and saying that we're doing it all for the kids when we've got scores below 90 percent of kids on benchmark!** It's like me saying, "I'm really eating healthily" – while I'm dipping french fries in ranch dressing with an ice cream cone in the other hand!

(That *does* sound good…but I digress!)

As responsible, professional educators **our actions needs to align with our talk**. If it's all about the kids – like *really* all about the kids – then we need to stop fighting adjustments and change. We need to put the hours that it takes to do the job completely in every day and every week. We need to try new strategies and when they *work*, keep doing them so that they become part of our regular teaching routines.

So here's **my question for you**: Where will you start (in your district or school or team) to move your colleagues and you toward talking about what the kids need instructionally, rather than what is convenient for the adults?

It's a habit that you *will* set. I just know it!

7
So What's Next?

Well, you've made it through Find Your Backbone 101. Your backbone is back there, strengthened and ready to work for you, if you'll let it. Using it to guide your work is like developing any new habit: the more you use it, the more natural using it becomes.

I said this in the Introduction of the book:

That's the thing:
When you principal with a backbone, you get results. Every time.

Here's the reality of it all: You know that one really, super-successful principal at the school in your district that gets all the accolades and awards?

Well that guy's got all of the same books that you have on your shelf. That guy's had all of the same training that you have. That guy's had all of the same resistance roll through his building that you have had. That guy's had the same number of hours in the day to get the job done that you have. That guy's had to fire people and hire people in the middle of the year, just like you. That guy's got raging bouts of insecurity and "What am I *doing*?" moments, just like you have.

But the difference is, he leads with a backbone.

When that guy reads the books that are on his shelf and decides to do something, he lays it out to his staff, gets them some support and then gets in the classrooms to make sure it's getting done. **That's a backbone at work.**

When that guy attends a training and recognizes a gap in what he's providing for kids, he goes back to school, pulls together his leadership team, shares the information and makes decisions about the one or two things that the staff needs to implement to combat that weakness. Then he gets in the classrooms to make sure it's getting done. **That's a backbone at work.**

When that guy overhears three of his teachers bad-mouthing the new literacy initiative by saying, "You know what? Our old program was working just fine." He asks those resistors to come into his office and he shares the schoolwide data that forced him to make those changes. **That's a backbone at work.**

When that guy is at the school until 9:00 p.m. for the fourth night in a row, he takes himself home and analyzes what on earth is keeping him there. When he realizes that his office staff is putting through every phone call and allowing people to just walk right into his office while he's working on his big project, he calls the office staff in and says, "Folks, we've got to clean this up and I need your help." **That's a backbone at work.**

When that guy realizes that the new teacher just isn't going to work and that there is no improvement after multiple conferences and coaching interactions, he calls his coach into the office and comes up with a contingency plan that'll go into effect immediately. **That's a backbone at work.**

When that guy is driving home from work that night after a contentious board meeting, with a pile of work that he didn't even make a dent in, and a slew of teachers who are out for conferences tomorrow, plus a voicemail from the district saying that there aren't enough subs to cover, he takes a deep breath and says, "Here we go! We can *do this*!" **That's a backbone at work.**

Your Final Assignment

Take out an index card right now. On the front, number 1-3. On the back number 1-3.

Note: Read these questions and immediately write your response on your index card – don't overthink it, don't overanalyze – just go with your gut.

On the front of the card next to #1, jot down your very short, very simple answer to this question:

What is my mission for this school year?

Next to #2, jot down your very short, very simple answer to this question:

Why is this mission important for our students?

Next to #3, jot down your very short, very simple answer to this question:

What is one word to describe what it will look like when we accomplish this mission?

Now turn the index card over.

Next to #1, jot down your very short, very simple answer to this question:

What is one word to describe what it will look like when you've accomplished the mission?

Next to #2, jot down your very short, very simple answer to this question:

Who are three people on my team who can help me on the mission?

Next to #3, jot down your very short, very simple answer to this question:

Who is one outside person who can help me on the mission and remind me of the big picture?

Fold the index card in half and put it in your wallet.

Now go to your calendar and in THREE PLACES, just make a note that says:

"Read index card".

When you principal with a backbone, you get results. Every time.

8
Resources

Resource #1: Three Tiered Goal Setting Template – District/School/Team, SAMPLE

Setting District Instructional Goals

	Description of Goal and What It Will Look Like When Accomplished	Check-in Dates with Principals
Goal #1	We will immediately implement information from our professional development sessions	10-10-12, 2-1-13, 5-3-13
Goal #2	Each site will agree upon a teaming schedule and organizational structure to make more efficient of early-release planning days	First admin meeting of every month
Goal #3	Administrators will complete weekly walk-throughs of each classroom with a specific goal for the observation and provide feedback to each teacher bi-monthly	Second admin meeting of every month

Setting School Instructional Goals

	Description of Goal and What It Will Look Like When Accomplished	Check-in Dates
Goal #1	We will hold a brief all-staff meeting following each professional development session where we will agree upon the "Top 3 Must Implements Right Away" steps from the training	9-30-12, 11-24-12, 2-10-13, 5-16-13
Goal #2	We will design a common team meeting recording sheet that will be used at every team meeting. We will hold each other accountable for full participation (according to our Non-Negotiables) and end each meeting with agreed upon "next steps" for every member of the team.	By October 30, 2012 Each teaming meeting
Goal #3	With the coach, we will set up monthly "look fors" for the principal to observe during regular walk-throughs. These "look fors" will match our school's instructional goals.	First team meeting of every month

Setting Team Instructional Goals

	Description of Goal and What It Will Look Like When Accomplished	Check-in Dates
Goal #1	During professional development, we will keep a running list of ideas that are a "stretch," a "can-do," and an "easy-to-implement." We will share these at our staff meetings.	9-30-12, 11-24-12, 2-10-13, 5-16-13
Goal #2	We will use our common team meeting recording sheet and rotate the roles during the meeting. Whoever is the "team lead" for that meeting is responsible for securing the agenda for the meeting and distributing all notes following the meeting. They will also lead the team in setting the next meeting's agenda.	By October 30, 2012

Each teaming meeting |
| Goal #3 | We will videotape our teaching 1x/month for 20 minutes during the implementation of our new(er) professional development learning. We will review these videos together every month and provide each other feedback. We will ask the coach to join us during these "movies" and to help us figure out what coaching support we need next. | Second team meeting of every month |

Resource #2: Three Tiered Goal Setting Template – District/School/Team

Setting District Instructional Goals

Description of Goal and What It Will Look Like When Accomplished	Check-in Dates
Goal #1	
Goal #2	
Goal #3	

Setting School Instructional Goals

	Description of Goal and What It Will Look Like When Accomplished	Check-in Dates
Goal #1		
Goal #2		
Goal #3		

Setting Team Instructional Goals

Description of Goal and What It Will Look Like When Accomplished	Check-in Dates
Goal #1	
Goal #2	
Goal #3	

Resource #3: Three Tiered Goal Setting Template – School/Team/Teacher

School Instructional Goals

	Description of Goal and What It Will Look Like When Accomplished	Check-in Dates
Goal #1		
Goal #2		
Goal #3		

Team Instructional Goals

Description of Goal and What It Will Look Like When Accomplished	Check-in Dates
Goal #1	
Goal #2	
Goal #3	

Teacher Instructional Goals

Description of Goal and What It Will Look Like When Accomplished	Check-in Dates
Goal #1	
Goal #2	
Goal #3	

Resource #4: Coaching Cycle Tracking Sheet, SAMPLE

Focus Area: Practice and Application

Provides hands-on materials and/or manipulatives for students to practice using new content knowledge. Uses activities that integrate all language skills ie: reading, writing, listening & speaking

Teacher	Date Pre-Conference	Focus for Coaching	Date Coached and Method of Coaching	Date Debriefed	Next Steps	Next Coaching Date	Notes
Jonny Johnson	9-12-12	Hands-on manips management	9-14-12 Observation	9-14-12	Set expectations for materials management so that materials do not become a distraction Design opportunities for students to explain how they used the manipulatives to learn the new concept – put it in their own words	9-19-12	Send reminder to set a time for us to get together to plan lesson for demo on 9-19-10 via email

Resource #5: Coaching Cycle Tracking Sheet

Focus Area:							
Teacher	Date Pre-Conference	Focus for Coaching	Date Coached and Method of Coaching	Date Debriefed	Next Steps	Next Coaching Date	Notes

Resource #6: Analyzing My Resistors

Who Are They	What Does It Look Like	What's Going Right	Possible Source of the Resistance	Three Next Steps	Support I'll Need Along the Way

Resource #7: Scripting the Conversation with My Biggest Resistor, SAMPLE

	Example	My script
Set the 'why' behind the conversation	Tabatha, I have brought you in today to resolve the on-going problem with you refusing to engage in work with our instructional coach. After this meeting, I will expect that you will begin to work with the coach, accepting feedback and implementing the suggestions and support. I have this same expectation of our entire staff. I will ask for your response following the information that I share with you.	
State the facts	I have witnessed you laughing and snickering during the presentations that our instructional coach has given during staff meetings. I have witnessed you being intentionally difficult and contrary as the coach works with your team, as well as defiant when the coach respectfully asks you to try a technique to increase the effectiveness of your teaching. I have seen no evidence that you have followed through on any of the recommendations of the coach.	

RESOURCES | 103

Share specific details of how the resistor's actions are affecting others	*You must know that the coach's work is directed by me and my desires for our staff, so by failing to implement her support, you are directly defying my expectations of you. You know, Tabatha, this is not the first time that we have discussed this and I have become increasingly frustrated by your refusal to comply.*	
	I have seen that your lack of follow-through and poor professional conduct has caused you to have a very negative attitude toward your teammates, our school and our district. This has affected your attitude with your students negatively, and I recognize almost daily that you are very short and impatient with our students. Your attitude is affecting your team, as several people have come to me concerned about working with you next year, due to your negativity.	

State your expectation	I realize that I should have come to you sooner to address these issues, as they are a true problem in your classroom, your team and our school. I give you my word that, I will speak with you sooner in the future, if necessary, to allow you to improve your behaviors and responses so that this does not get to this point again.	
Expected steps and timeline	Tabatha I am asking you to completely cease mocking the coaching role and to comply with my expectation that each teacher willingly work with the coach on an ongoing basis.	

Firm consequences	*If you choose to continue this behavior, your choice will force me to start you on an improvement plan that, if carried out to the fullest, will result in you losing your job.*	
Gutsy closing	*My desire is to resolve this issue immediately so that we can restore our focus on the instruction of our students. I know that you can do this and I am willing to support you in any way that is appropriate to help you remedy these problems.*	

Resource #8: Scripting the Conversation with My Biggest Resistor

	Example	My script
Set the 'why' behind the conversation		
State the facts		
Share specific details of how the resistor's actions are affecting others		
State your expectation		

Expected steps and timeline		
Firm consequences		
Gutsy Closing		

Acknowledgements

To Mom, Dad, Beebe, Sissy and Elliot: Thank you for teaching me to do my thing and always encouraging me to do it. I could never, ever thank you enough for your support, your love, your teasing, your patience, your general hilariousness and how well you take care of me.

To Cricket: Thank you for being the best friend a girl could ever dream of and also for bringing your talents, your tenaciousness and your dedication to what we do every day. I couldn't have done half of what I do in life without you in my corner. And to think it all began with one girl with a run-on problem and the other who was the opposite of graceful.

To Toni Dunbar: Thank you for seeing in me something I didn't see in myself when I was a brand-spanking-new teacher, and for encouraging me to go into this side of the education field. It's because of you I know this side exists! You are as powerful now to me as you were back then, and it is a dream realized to be learning under you yet again.

To Linda Diamond: Thank you for managing my audaciousness and taking me under your wing when, at times, I probably didn't deserve it. You toughened me up, gave me a stage to try new things and taught me to get my facts straight. I count my years working with you as my most formative.

Extra big thanks to Eric Yates and Karla Buffington for helping me write as if I actually graduated from fifth grade.

To all of the teachers who bring their best every day, especially to the kids who many think don't stand a chance; my hat is off to you.